Taking Root in Rocky Soil

3,000 Years of Art in the Wind River Mountains

by Bob Bahr

CONTENTS

Acknowledgements   3

Chapter 1   The Winds: Remote and Enchanting   9

Chapter 2   Crossroads: The Wind River Mountains
                 and the Mixing of Cultures   32

Chapter 3   Spirits in the Cracks of Rocks   44

Chapter 4   Early Explorers, Trappers, and Alfred
                 Jacob Miller: Undiscovered Country   68
                 (1742-1849)

Chapter 5   Artists and Manifest Destiny: Bierstadt
                 and the Surveying Expeditions   87
                 (1843-1890)

Chapter 6   The Modern Era: "My Heart Was in the
                 West" (1890-present)   99

Bibiliography   132

Index   138

Acknowledgements

Thank you to the Susan Kathleen Black Foundation founder, Jim Parkman; executive director, Pam Cable; and its board of directors. Thanks to Meredith and Tory Taylor, Stephen V. Banks, Peter H. Hassrick, and Clint Gilchrist. Thanks to the following for always helping when I wanted to pick their brains: John Phelps, John Finley, Monie Finley, Tammy Lucas, Tom Lucas, Leon Sanderson, Mike and Jenn Slider, Bob Koenke, and James Coe. Thank you to Bonnie Smith at the Buffalo Bill Center of the West, and Joe Brandl, a man who knows his way around the Winds. Thank you, Sean Berthelot, for the wonderful cover design. Thanks to my wife, Lynne Moss Bahr, for corralling the kids each year while I'm in Wyoming and for reading my text with a wife's unflinching honesty and an editor's sharp eyes, and thank you to Steve Doherty for being snowed under with deadlines in 2007, and sending me in his stead to report on the Dubois workshop. Look what you did…

This book is dedicated to my father, Louis A. Bahr, Jr., who was the role model for me as a journalist, as a visual artist, and as a person with never-quenched curiosity.

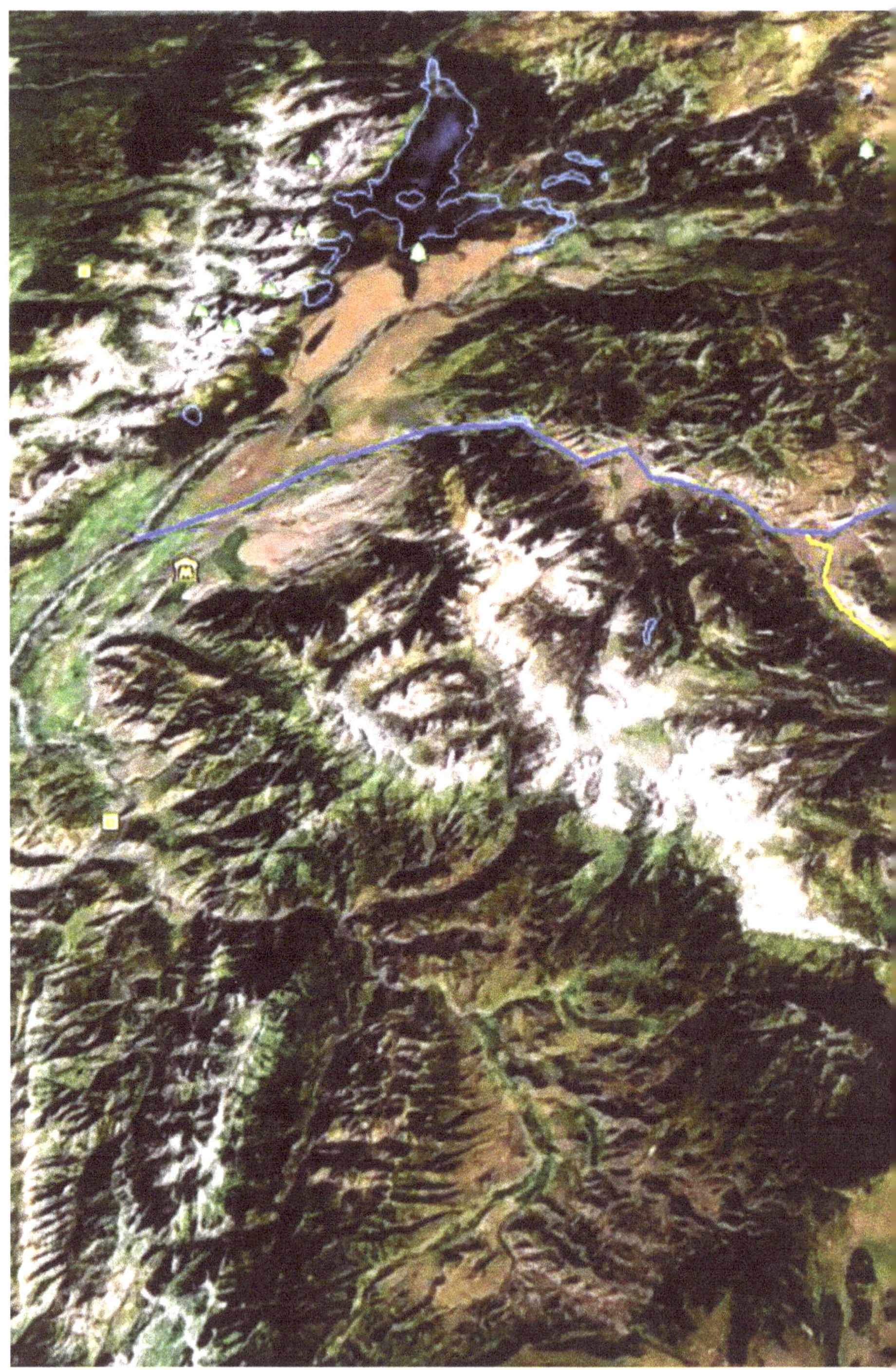

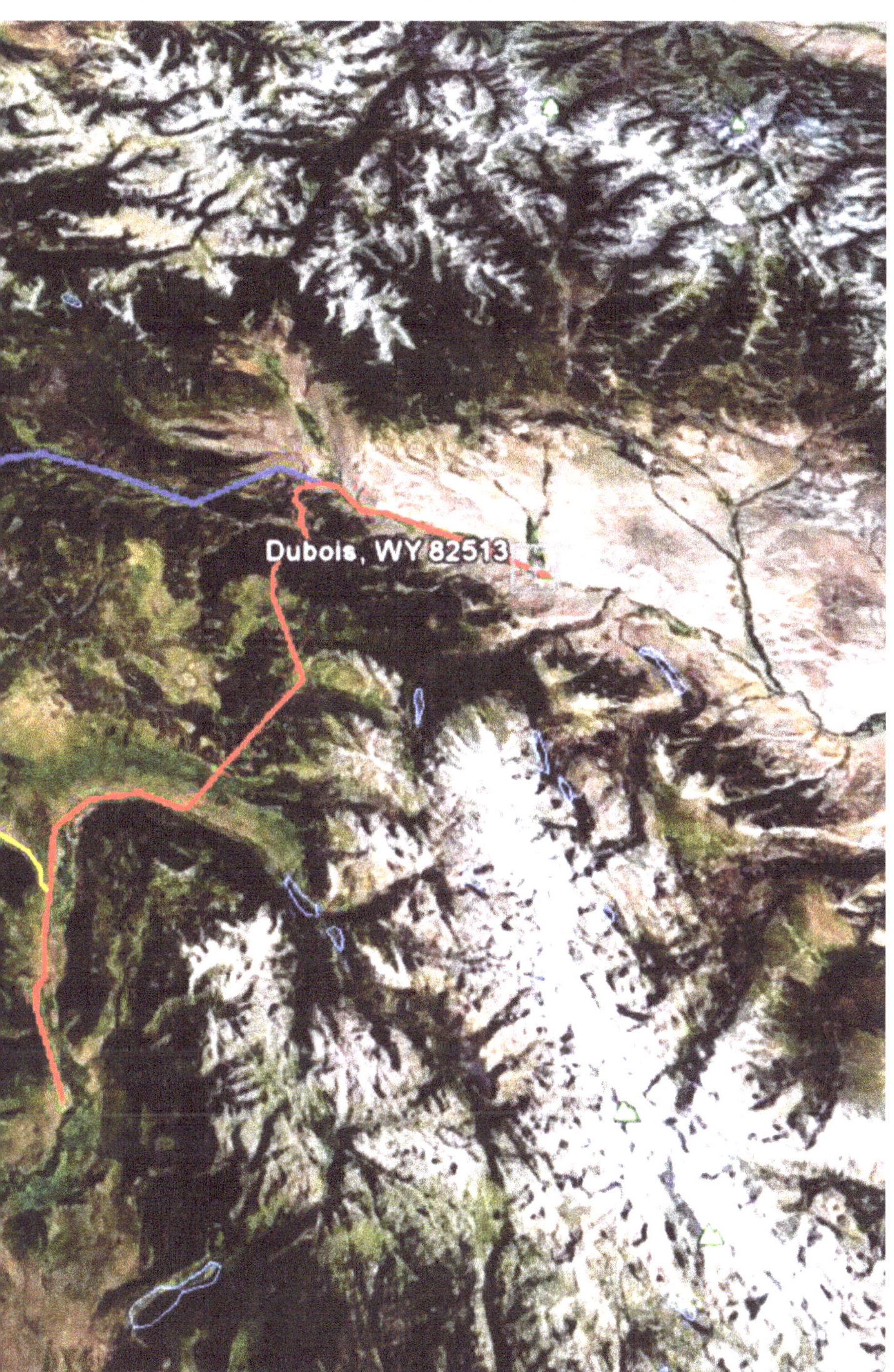

Dubois, WY 82513

I am as much convinced as ever that the immense Rocky Mountain states represent as clear an expression of the undefined, and I suppose, undefinable, American wish as you can find. And because they are so clear-cut and themselves, and yet so native and indigenous, I am equally convinced that they will continue indefinitely to refresh spiritually any American who will seek them out and get to know them.

– *Maxwell Struthers Burt,* The Diary of a Dude Wrangler, *1938, Charles Scribner's Sons, NYC*

The Wind River Area, Wyoming

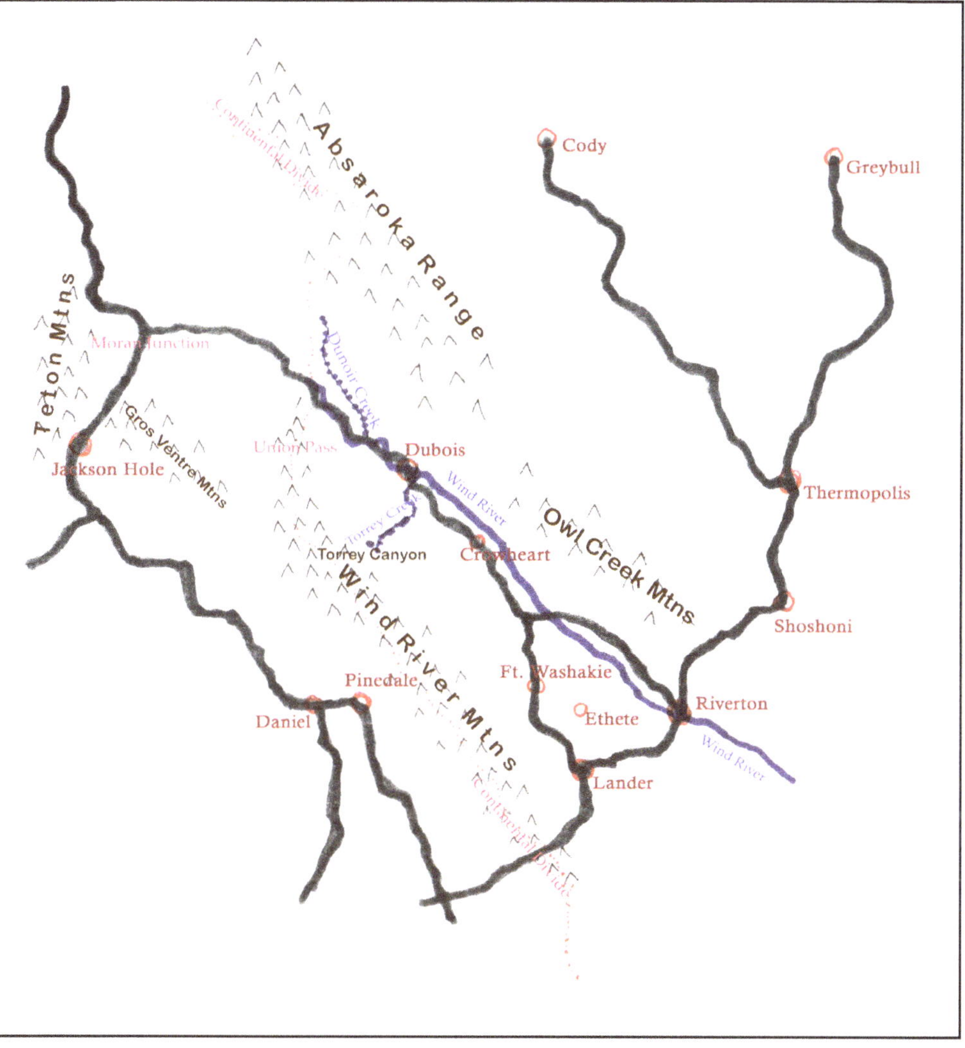

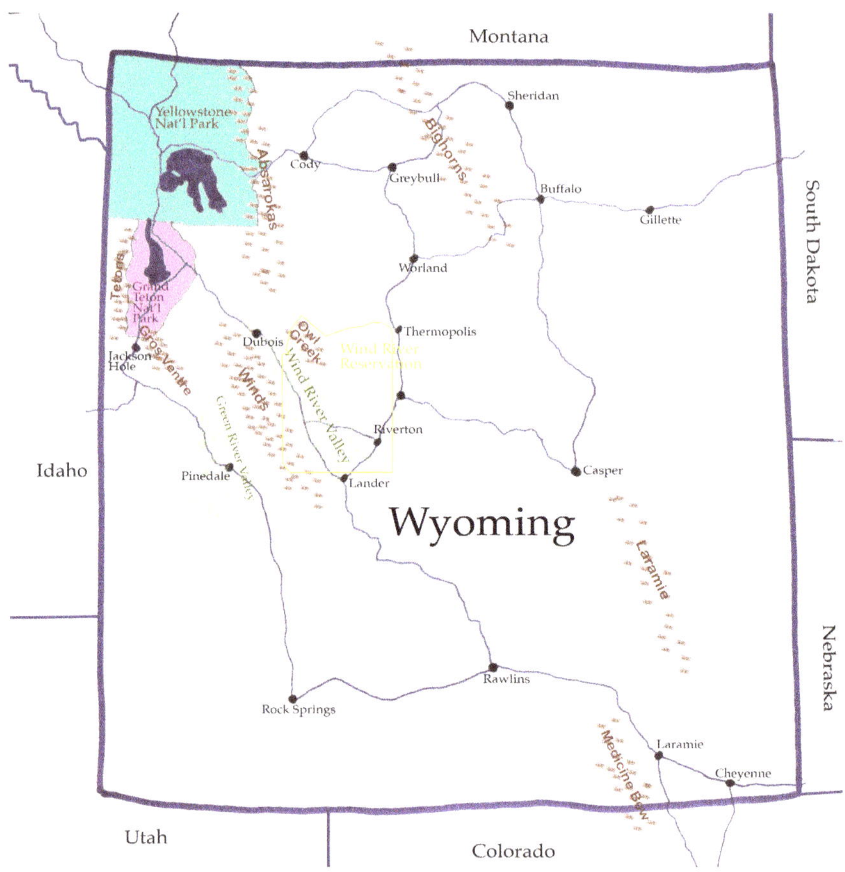

Montana
Idaho
Utah
Colorado
Nebraska
South Dakota
Wyoming
Yellowstone Nat'l Park
Grand Teton Nat'l Park
Wind River Reservation
Absarokas
Bighorns
Tetons
Gros Ventre
Winds
Owl Creek
Wind River Valley
Green River Valley
Laramie
Medicine Bow
Sheridan
Cody
Greybull
Buffalo
Gillette
Worland
Thermopolis
Dubois
Jackson Hole
Riverton
Casper
Pinedale
Lander
Rawlins
Rock Springs
Laramie
Cheyenne

Chapter 1

The Winds: Remote and Enchanting

Why should a book on the history of visual arts in the Wind River Mountains and its valleys be written? What is there to learn about arts in this rugged land? What could possibly motivate hard-bitten explorers, leather-skinned cowboys and cowgirls, and the spiritually and martially oriented Native Americans to take time to draw, paint, craft, and build? Why has art always found a way to thrive in a country that can punish any human who miscalculates what is needed for basic survival? There are many questions for the curious sort to ask. Let's try to answer as many as we can.

Why the Winds?

"Colorado has the mountains and timber. Utah has the canyons and red rock. Idaho has timbered hills and some of the sagebrush flats—and the Rocky Mountains. But there are not too many places that have everything.

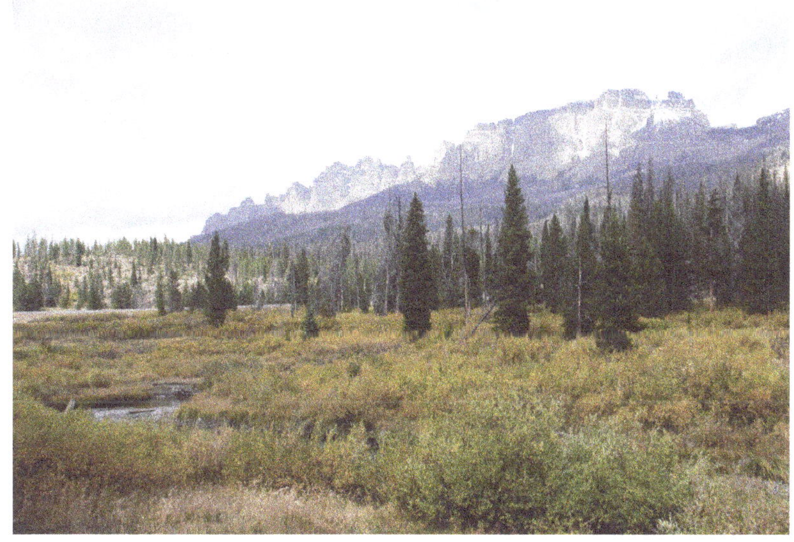

The Pinnacles in fall, near Brooks Lake close to Togwotee Pass. Area rancher John Finley says, "The Wind River Valley draws a lot of artists. It has everything—a bit of Colorado, Utah, Idaho—all the different landscapes are right here in Dubois."

This place does."

John Finley's family has lived in the Dubois area of Wyoming since 1901, but he's rarely been asked the question of the Wind River Mountains' appeal, it seems. Over a dinner along the Wind River, he and his wife, Monie, pondered the question. John answered with the above, then went on, addressing why he works as a rancher, an accomplished craftsman, a guide, and an artist who paints watercolors, makes saddles, scrimshaw, paintings on wasp's nests, and full-size sculptures, all in a place that can punish the lax and even the steadfast.

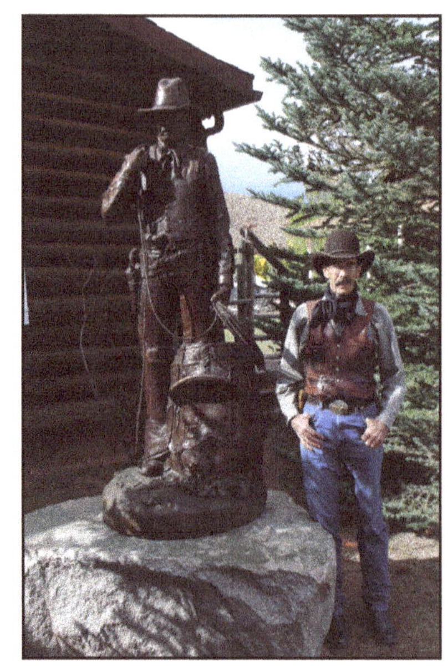

"Growing up here, I guess I've taken everything for granted," he said. "I'm an artist, but I don't know if it is the landscape I grew up in that turned me into one, or if I would have been an artist anyway. But there are quite a few artists who have moved here; the Wind River Valley draws a lot of artists. It has everything—a bit of Colorado, Utah, Idaho—all the different landscapes are right here in Dubois, all right here in one little spot. Some of the ridges, like

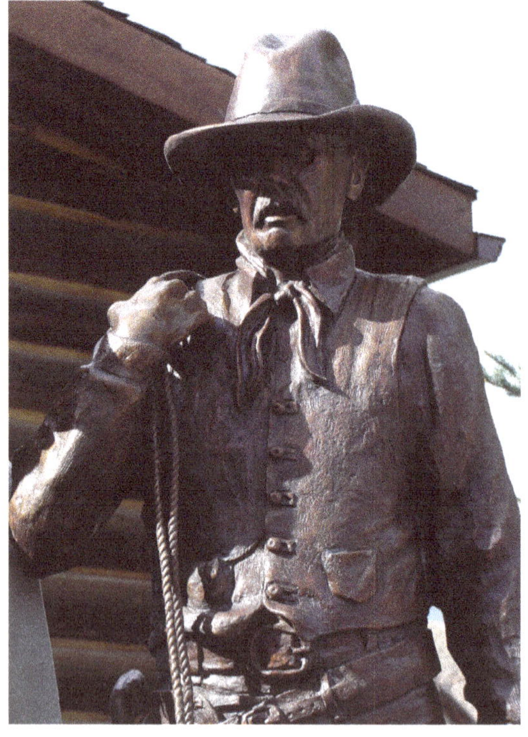

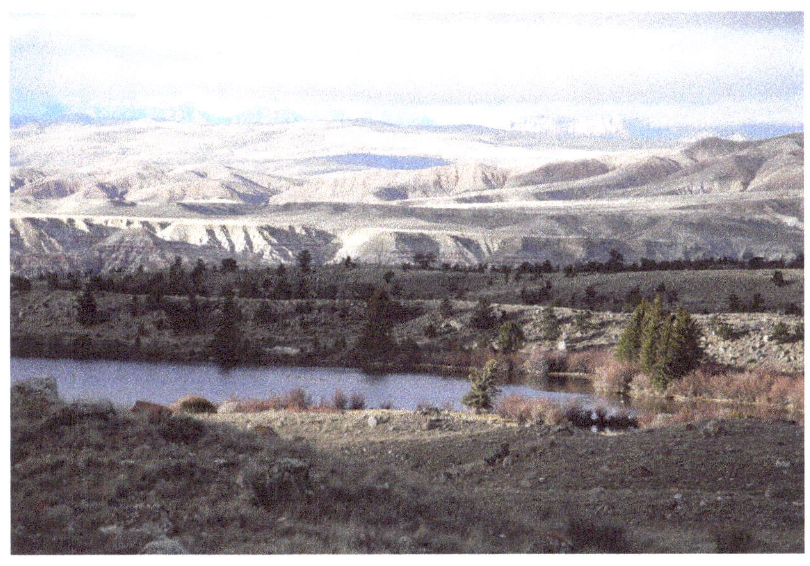

View looking northeast from Whiskey Basin.

the one behind my house, turn pink and other very different colors as they catch the evening sun. Not many ranges anywhere else run from northeast to southwest and catch that late light. These things are what the Upper Wind River Valley has that nowhere else has."

Monie, who also works the ranch and was a longtime guiding force at the National Bighorn Sheep Interpretive Center in Dubois, agreed. "Some of the dudes I used to ride with were impressed with the diversity of the landscapes," she said. "They found them all scenic and interesting, but different—and they were very impressed by that."

The Finleys and the dudes they've met are not alone in this opinion. A geologist named David Love chose a section of land centered on the Absaroka Range as the subject of his Yale Ph.D. thesis in the late 1930s. John McPhee, in his Pulitzer Prize-winning book *Annals of the Former World*, writes, "[Love's] thesis area reached a short distance into the Wind

Opposing page: John Finley with his sculpture "Western Knight" which sits outside of the historic Dennison Lodge in Dubois, Wyoming. Finley used his grandfather's saddle as a model for the saddle in the piece, and the 7' cowboy figure was originally a small chess piece Finley made as part of a Western-themed set.

River Basin, and thus completed in its varied elements the panoply of the Rockies. It included folded mountains and dissected plateaus. It included basin sediments and alpine peaks, dry gulches and superposed master streams, desert sageland and evergreen forest rising to a timberline at 10,400 feet. … at any given place in the area, temperatures could change 80 degrees in less than a day."

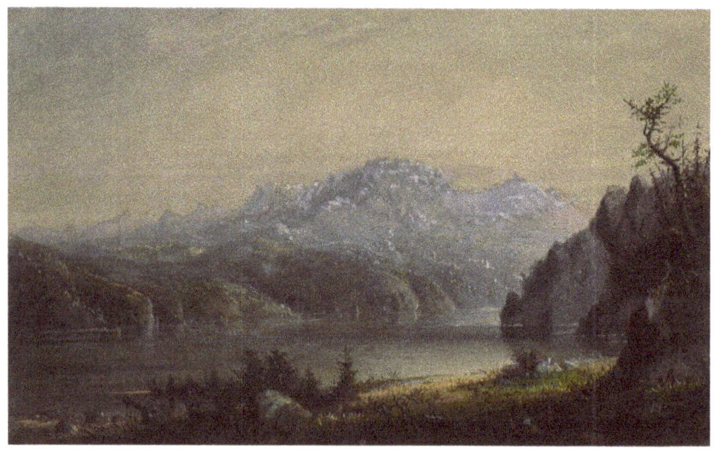

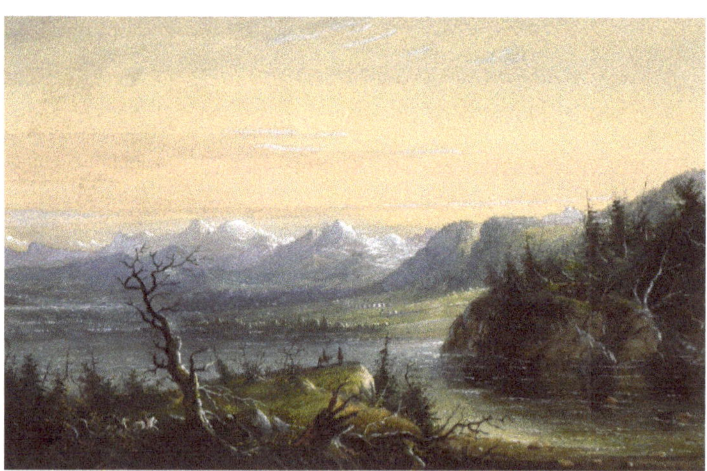

Top: "Lake Scene, Wind Mountains," by Alfred Jacob Miller,
1858, watercolor, 18 x 29 ¼ in.

Bottom: "Wind River Chain," by Alfred Jacob Miller,
1858, watercolor, 8 ½ x 12 ½ in. Collection of
the Walters Art Museum, Baltimore.

Early visitors from the East reached for comparisons to the Swiss Alps and other known mountain ranges in Europe and in the eastern half of the United States. It was quite a reach, indeed. Someone acquainted with the Alps would be startled by the high mountain meadows, a remnant from when ash and sediment filled the valleys nearly to the tops of the Winds. One could walk from peak to peak on relatively level land. Worn by wind and water erosion, the Wind River Mountains mix the occasional craggy peak and rock cliff with smooth, rolling summits. Just to their southwest, the Tetons scratch the clouds with their youthful profiles. The Winds belong to an older geological event than the Tetons' geologically recent rise to the skies.

Where did the Wind River Mountains come from?

Says McPhee about the Winds, the Laramie, the Owl Creek, the Bighorn,

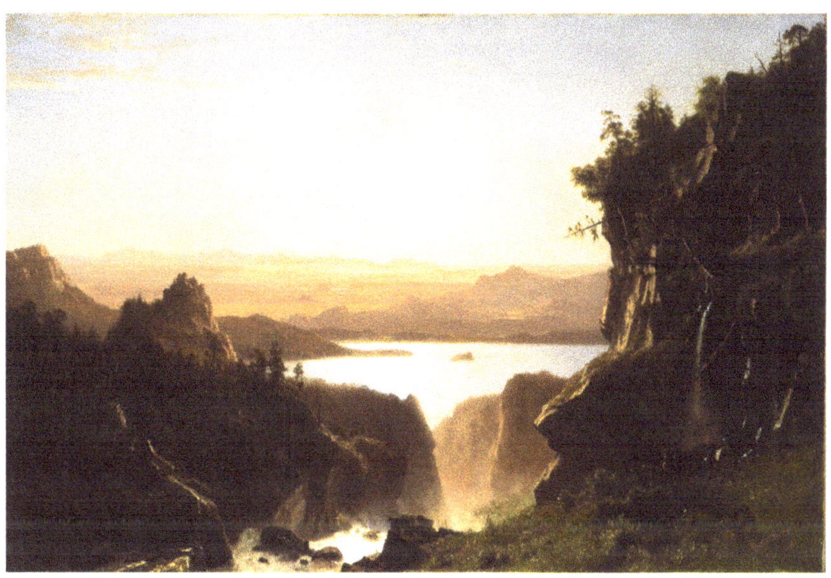

"Island Lake, Wind River Range, Wyoming," by Albert Bierstadt,
1861, oil, 26 ½ x 40 ½ in.
Famed painter Albert Bierstadt wrote a missive back to New York while visiting the Winds, and said, "We see many spots in the scenery that remind us of our New Hampshire and Catskills hills, but when we look up and measure the mighty perpendicular cliffs that rise hundreds of feet aloft, all capped with snow, we then realize that we are among a different class of mountains, especially when we see the antelope stop to look at us."

the Uinta, and the Medicine Bow mountains of Wyoming, "All these mountain ranges were coming up out of the craton—heartland of the continent, the Stable Interior Craton [craton: old and stable interior part of a tectonic plate]. It was as if mountains had appeared in Ohio, inboard of the Appalachian thrust sheets, like a family of hogs waking up beneath a large blanket. An authentic enigma on a grand scale, this was one of the oddest occurrences in the tectonic history of the world. It would probe anybody's theories." Their uprising is called the Laramide Orogeny.

McPhee goes on to explain that mountains are constantly fighting a battle of orogeny (creation) and erosion (destruction). When the Winds were "born," they rose 60,000 feet above the surrounding rock.

Volcanoes came next, starting around 50 million years ago, and they buried the ranges in ash, to the point where the Owl Creek

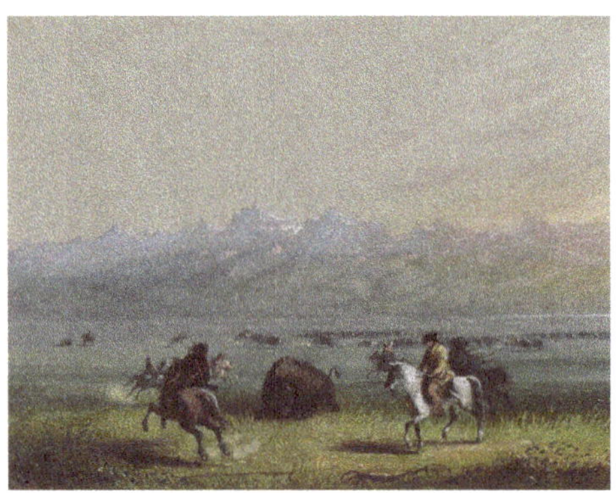

"Wounded Buffalo," by Alfred Jacob Miller, 1858, watercolor, 9 ¼ x 12 ¼ in. Collection of the Walters Art Museum, Baltimore.

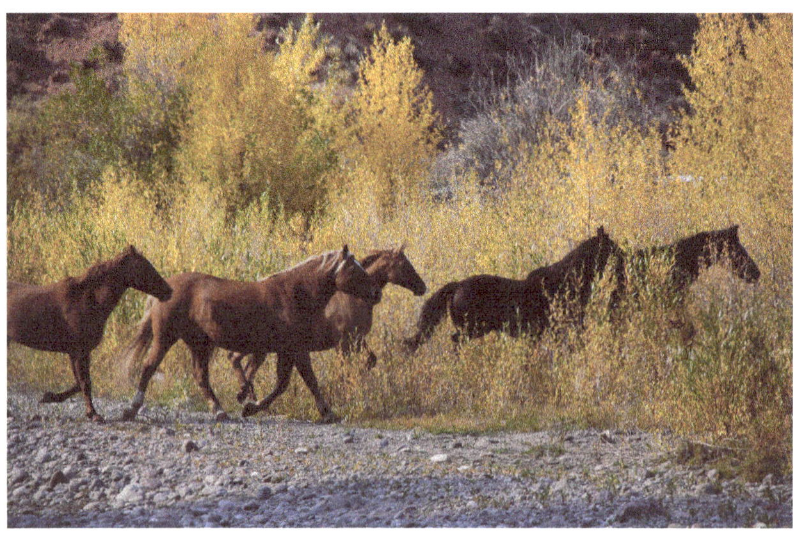

Horses on the Finley Ranch.

Mountains were only 1,000-4,000 feet tall, and the rivers were clogged with volcanic ash falling from the sky from eruptions hundreds of miles away—from as far as Oregon. Volcanic sand, blown by the wind, piled up in Central Wyoming, and as Jackson became Jackson Hole, the depression was partially filled with this sand.

Then, about 10 million years ago, a deep internal force in the Earth's crust pushed the better part of Wyoming up, and the rivers that had flowed methodically through the region were rerouted as they rushed down the mountainsides, pushed by gravity. The rivers picked up boulders that acted like "teeth of a saw," as McPhee puts it. The force was strong enough to break mountain passes in ranges, and urge rivers to take unusual courses. (Consider the course of the Bighorn River or the Wind River, to see this effect. Flowing east, then north, then curling—these rivers defied expectations and confused explorers and even some indigenous people.) This event is called the Exhumation of the Rockies. "While rivers elsewhere, running in their dendritic patterns like the veins in a leaf, shape in harmony the landscapes they dominate, almost all the rivers of the Rockies seem to argue with nature as well as with common sense. … The Wind River addresses itself to the Owl Creek Mountains and flows right at them," McPhee writes. "It breaks through and comes out the other side. It flowed across the totally buried mountains in the Miocene Epoch, and

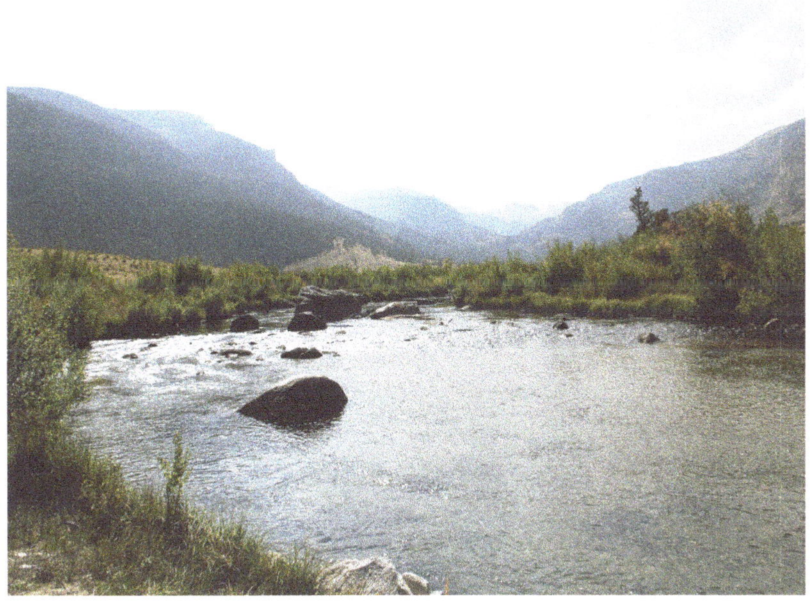

Torrey Canyon

descended upon them during the exhumation. The anomaly is so startling that early explorers, and even aborigines, did not put one and one together. To the waters on the south side of the mountains they gave the name Wind River. The waters on the north side they called the Bighorn."

Why are they called the Winds?

McPhee refers to the Wind River Mountains as "the supreme expression in Wyoming of the Laramide Orogeny." They are not just supreme, but also extreme, remote, enchanting. Early trappers called the Wind River Valley "Warmland" because of its mild winters. The Shoshone allegedly called it Warm Valley. The relatively temperate summers led early settlers to call Dubois, located in the Upper Wind River Valley, "Never Sweat," but the U.S. postal service balked at the name and called it Dubois after an Idaho senator. John Finley jokes that the winding, twisting, and turning waterway "used to be the 'wind' river [as in a winding road] until all the people came here and mispronounced it, and suddenly it was windy." Of course, the running joke in Wyoming is that no one ever talks about the wind unless it stops. THAT is news.

Why are the Winds still remote?

The Winds never did get the publicity that adjacent areas enjoyed. Yellowstone National Park is an international travel destination. The Teton Mountains are breathtaking in their almost surreal thrust upward, revealing

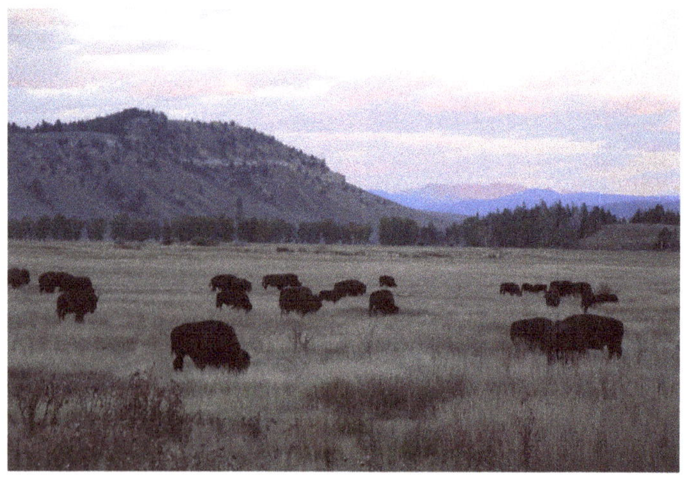

Bison, with the Wind River Mountains in the distance.

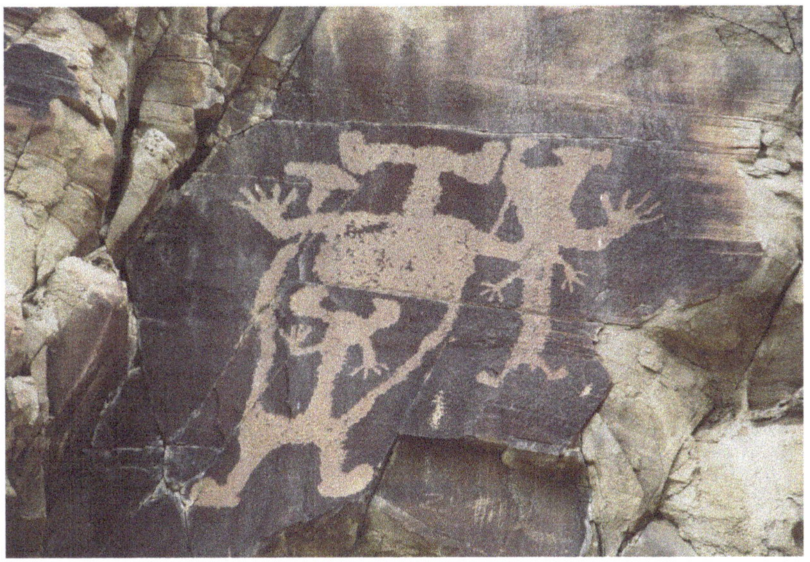

Petroglyphs from Legend Rock, located outside of Thermopolis, Wyoming.

stark cliffs and iconic summits when viewed from the East. "Only Maxfield Parrish could paint [the Tetons], and he makes his mountains up," writes Struthers Burt.

The Winds quietly keep their untamed nature, their anomalous origins largely unknown, their backcountry nearly empty for intrepid outdoor fans to enjoy their fruits away from crowds. Tranquil mountain lakes, trout-stuffed streams, bear country and elk migrations, bighorn sheep grazing along dirt or gravel roads, eagles and osprey, foxes and badgers, moose and ground squirrels—the Winds are still quite wild.

Modern day hunters, fly fishermen, ATV enthusiasts, and hikers appreciate the Wind River Mountains. The Crow and the Shoshone tribes long tussled over hunting rights in the Winds, showing that they understood the area's wealth of resources. But some of the early explorers and surveyors seemed to both recognize and look past the appeal of the Wind River Mountains. Andrew A. Humphreys ventured West with a charge from the U.S. Government to find a route for a transcontinental railroad, and his impression of the Winds was simply that the valley was "a favorable wintering place." William F. Raynolds called the Wind River Valley "unproductive" but in the next sentence said, "The mountains upon either side are bold and lofty, and present a constant succession of striking landscapes."

Famed painter Albert Bierstadt wrote a missive back to New York while visiting the Winds, and said, "We see many spots in the scenery that remind us of our New Hampshire and Catskills hills, but when we look up and measure the mighty perpendicular cliffs that rise hundreds of feet aloft, all capped with snow, we then realize that we are among a different class of mountains, especially when we see the antelope stop to look at us." The first superintendent of Yellowstone National Park, Nathaniel P. Langford, encountered the Winds as part of the Washburn expedition of 1870. He wrote, "The mountain on which we stood was the most westerly peak of a range which, in long-extended volume, swept to the southeastern horizon, exhibiting a continuous elevation more than 30 miles in width; its central line broken into countless points, knobs, glens, and defiles, all on the most colossal scale of grandeur and magnificence."

Why aren't they more developed by humans?

As far back as 1832, the artist George Catlin recognized the need to

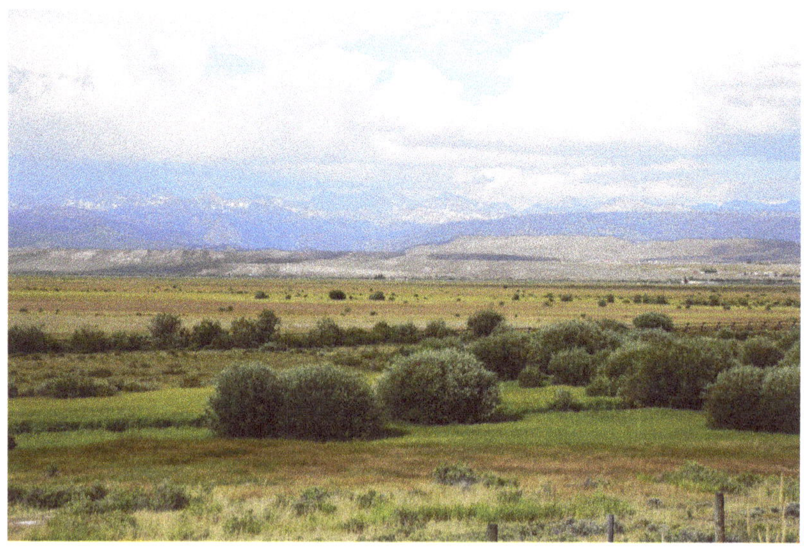

South side of the Wind River. Whiskey Basin is within the Wind River Mountains, which represent a buckling of the Earth's crust, and their makeup is sedimentary rock. Across the Wind River Valley, the Absarokas and the Dubois Badlands are igneous rock, bubbled and shot from volcanoes.

appreciate and preserve the wildness of the West. Peter H. Hassrick, in *Albert Bierstadt: Witness to a Changing West,* wrote how Catlin's writings advocated "a bold solution. Why not, he dreamed, succumb to a 'splendid contemplation,' imagining 'them as they might in future be seen (by some great protecting policy of the government) preserved in their pristine beauty and wildness, in a magnificent park'? Why not have the United States 'hold up to the view of her refined citizens and the world, in future ages! A nation's Park, containing man and beast, in all the wild and freshness of their nature's beauty'?"

"Caitlin's plea did prove, however, that artists at least were trying to shape America's conversation about the West and its denizens, both animal and human. Caitlin's remonstrations about the inexorable advance of civilization beseeched the nation to consider the extraordinary qualities of the region and the synergistic existence of those who lived in America's most remote wilderness."

The Wind River mountains and valley are now largely protected, not as national parks, but as designated wilderness areas, national forests, and as land under the stewardship of the Native Americans on the Wind River Reservation.

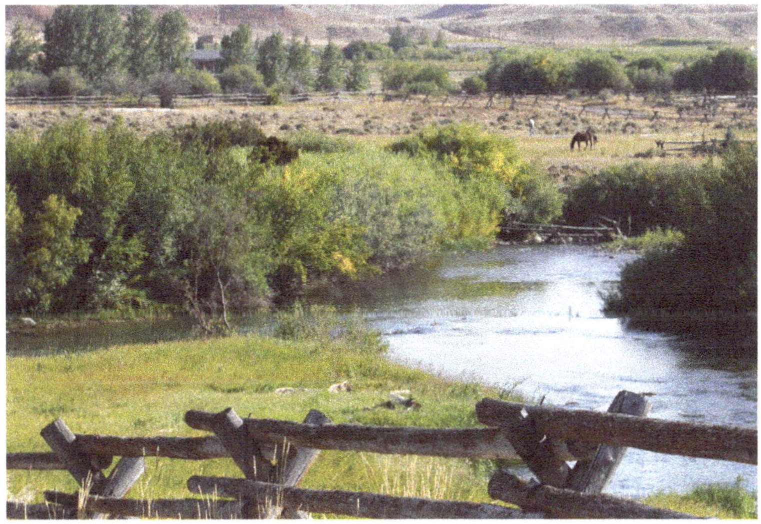

"Development" in the Winds still mostly refers to ranches and similarly minimal changes to the land.

Why such notable art-making
in the Wind River Mountains?

Living in Wyoming away from its 13 or so good-sized cities makes for a rugged life. (Almost 50% of Wyomingites live outside of those towns.) Many people have more than one job, and also maintain property that may graze cattle, host tourists, or at the very least, stable horses. There's a lot of work to be done. It's hard to imagine that things were any easier for the indigenous people who have inhabited the area for more than 10,000 years. And yet visual art has been a mainstay in the Winds and its two main valleys—the Wind River Valley and the Green River Valley.

"There's something about this area," John Finley says. "Even the early people here, the Native Americans, for some reason they were inspired and wanted to create and leave something that was an artistic statement. If my dad hadn't sold a lot of the ranch off, I probably wouldn't have time for art—it would have been all up to me to run it. My older brother was pushed

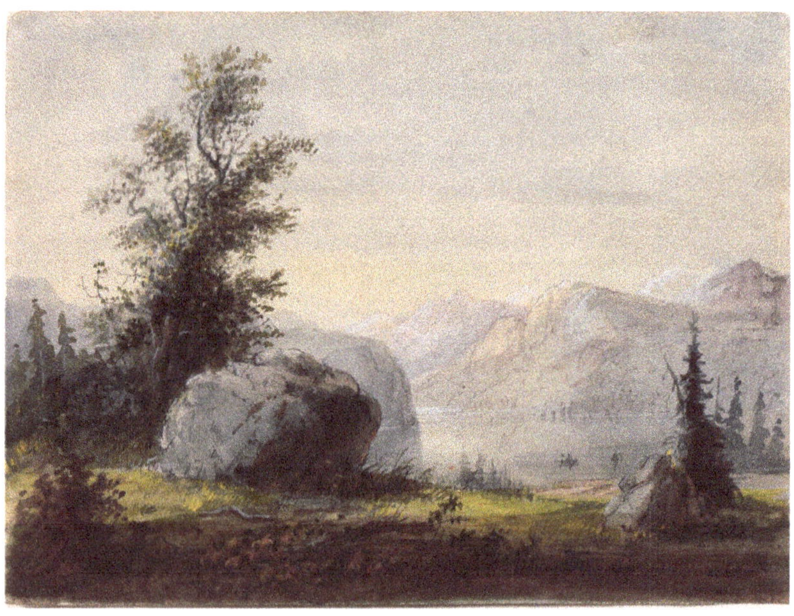

"Lake—Wind River" by Alfred Jacob Miller, goauche.
Some of the most famous painters of their day depicted the mountains of northwest
Wyoming and declared them on par with Europe's Alps.

out of ranching by allergies. My other brother became a logger and was artistic; he did art in high school. And he was president of the Wind River Valley Artists' Guild at times."

It's about the land. People everywhere tend to be proud of where they live, but folks in the Winds seem to go further and attach themselves to the landscape in a way most people don't. Being in the Wind River Mountains is revitalizing. It's stimulating. It's beautiful.

"The Wind River Mountains are, in fact, among the most remarkable of the whole Rocky chain; and would appear to be among the loftiest," writes Washington Irving in his *The Adventures of Captain Bonneville*. "They form, as it were, a great bed of mountains, … with rugged peaks, covered with eternal snows, and deep, narrow valleys, full of springs, and brooks, and rock-bound lakes. From this great treasury of waters issue forth limpid streams, which, augmenting as they descend, become main tributaries of the Missouri on the one side, and the Columbia on the other; and give rise to the Green River, the Colorado of the West, that empties its current into the Gulf of California. … The Wind River Mountains are notorious in hunters' and trappers' stories: their rugged defiles, and the rough tracts about their neighborhood, having been lurking places for the predatory hordes of the mountains, and scenes of rough encounter with Crows and Blackfeet."

Over the next five chapters, we'll explore the allure of the Winds, their history, and the indomitable art spirit that continues to thrive and compel people to make art in one of the most rugged and wild places on the continent.

Chapter 2

Crossroads: The Wind River Mountains and the Mixing of Cultures

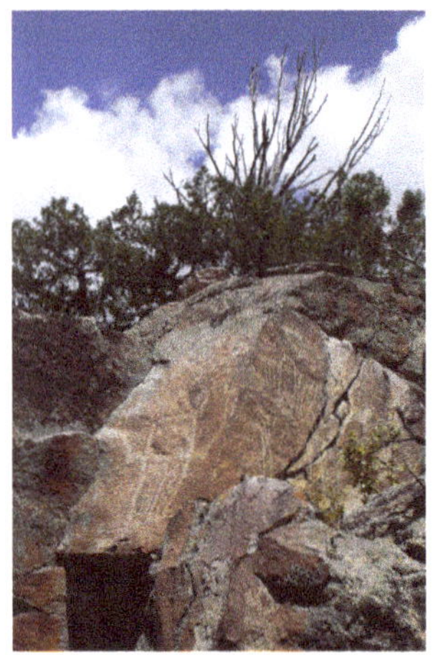

In a 20-mile wide swath of grand peaks and foothills that runs in Wyoming from Union Pass nearly 100 miles southeast, past Lander almost to Atlantic City, humans, sheep, elk, antelope, and other animals migrated for thousands of years, hunting, grazing, and making art, exploring and settling in for a season. The area's wild mountains captivated their hearts, toughened their hides, honed their skills. The Wind River Mountains and the river valleys on either side of them—the Green River Valley and the Wind River Valley—constitute a crossroads of cultures, habitats, geological events, and industry. And from Paleolithic times, humans have commented on life in the Winds through visual art.

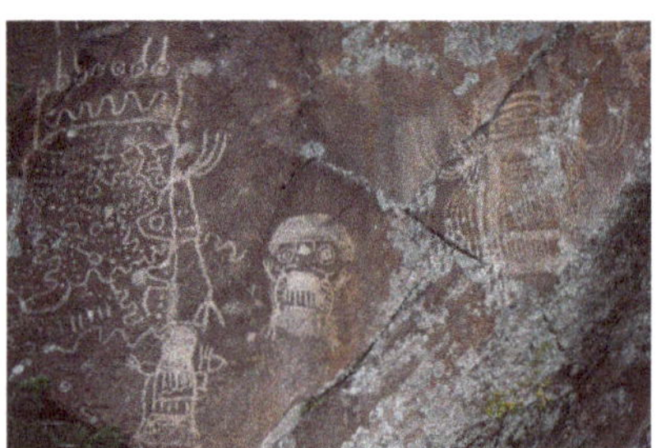

The Wind River Mountains, along with the Gros Ventre, Absaroka, and Teton ranges, sparked wonder and

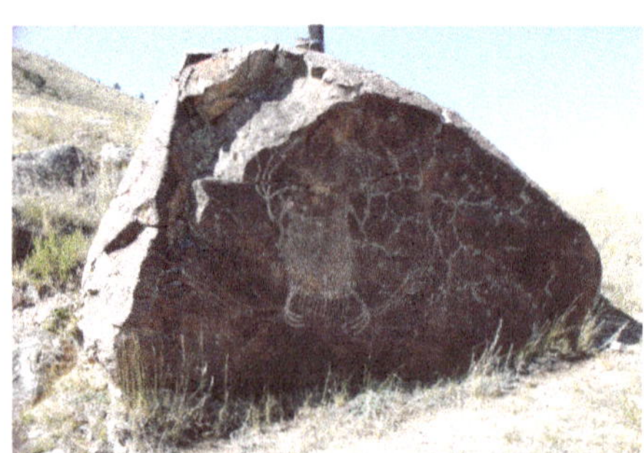

Dotting Torrey Canyon in various spots are petroglyphs, images pecked into the stone using a point. Their meaning and origin are unknown. The images are mysterious. It's not clear if they were done over thousands of years, or in one era. Their purpose has been debated for decades.

nationalistic pride in white explorers and trappers from the East during the 1800s. Some of the most famous painters of their day depicted the mountains of northwest Wyoming and declared them on par with Europe's Alps. But art was created in the Winds long before Albert Bierstadt came around. To plumb this history, we must go to Whiskey Basin, a depression gouged out by glaciers, and marked today by Torrey, Ring, and Trail lakes.

That relatively low land—it's still at 7,000 feet above sea level—is bordered by two very different types of rock. Whiskey Basin is within the Wind River Mountains, which represent a buckling of the Earth's crust, and their makeup is sedimentary rock. Across the Wind River Valley, the Absarokas and the Dubois Badlands are igneous rock, bubbled and shot from volcanoes. Whiskey Basin starts in Torrey Canyon, "behind" Whiskey Mountain, and runs south by southeast before curving into the three lakes area. Glaciers pushed down from the north through the basin, leaving glacial erratics (big boulders originating hundreds of miles away) atop the hills. The moraines— the buildup of sediment pushed to the extreme end of the glaciers—lie

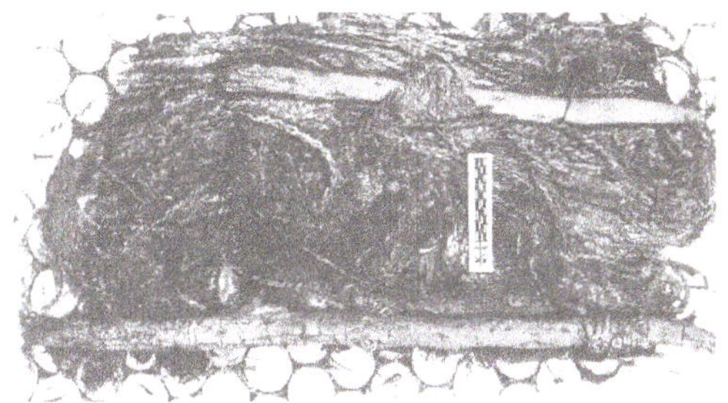

The wide weave of this net, which dates back 8,800 years, suggests it was used on large game such as bighorn sheep (below).

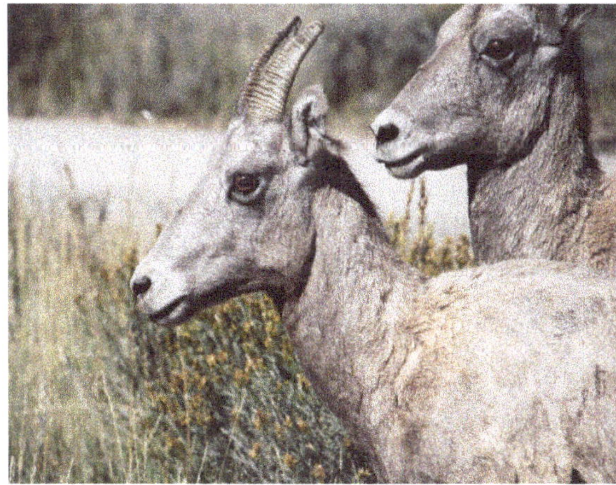

Even today, Whiskey Basin hosts 1,200 bighorn sheep, the largest population of bighorn sheep in the world. It's no wonder the name Sheep Eater has stuck, even in the face of mitigating evidence.

between Whiskey Basin and Highway 26, just east of Dubois.

Those lobes of ice extending from the glaciers scraped the sedimentary rocks of Whiskey Mountain and left glacial erratics (boulders carried by the glacier) and flattened faces of sandstone, usually looking down into the basin. These provided an ideal surface for prehistoric people to make their marks.

Dotting Torrey Canyon in various spots are petroglyphs, images pecked into the stone using a point. Their meaning and origin are unknown. The images are mysterious. Some have outstretched limbs that resemble wings. Others look like some sort of alien creature. There are beetle-like shapes, and in nearby areas, the occasional herd animal. Lines emanate from some figures, like filaments or waves of power. It's not clear if they were done over thousands of years, or in one era. Their purpose has been debated for decades.

Regardless, they represent the earliest art in the Wind River Range. Some publications casually label the petroglyphs the work of the Sheep Eater Indians, a Native American clan that is an offshoot of the Eastern

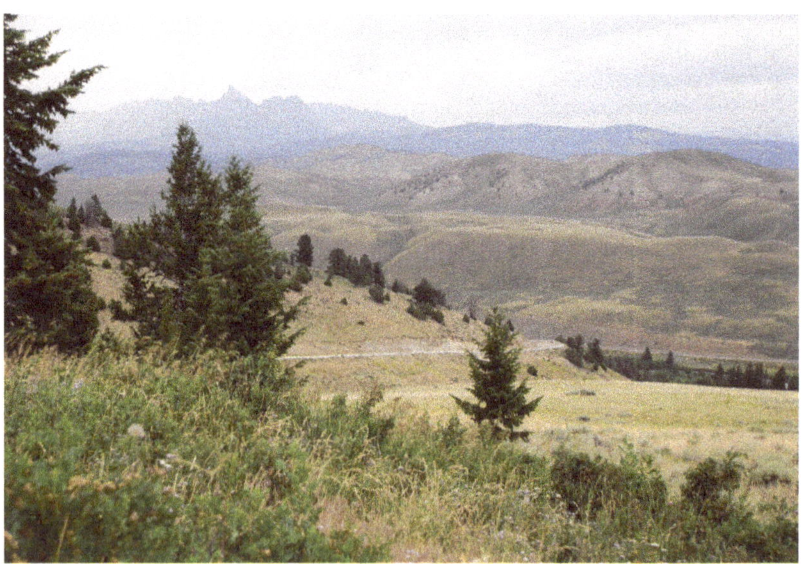

View from Union Pass. The Wind River Mountains and the river valleys on either side of them—the Green River Valley and the Wind River Valley—constitute a crossroads of cultures, habitats, geological events, and industry. And from Paleolithic times, humans have commented on life in the Winds through visual art.

Shoshone. The very term Sheep Eater has been challenged, however. Tory Taylor, a Dubois historian who has served as a guide for anthropological and archaeological expeditions in the upper reaches of the Wind River Mountains, says the name "Sheep Eater" is a bit of a misnomer. Other clans ate sheep, and the Sheep Eaters ate more than just sheep. Evidence found in archaeological digs, such as High Rise Village, show that the early inhabitants of the Winds also ate pine nuts, rose hips, and grains. The early inhabitants, dated at least back 3,000 years, spoke Numic, the root of a number of later Native American tongues, including Shoshone, Comanche, and Ute. For simplicity's sake, with a nod to accuracy, Taylor prefers the term Mountain Shoshone.

Referring to this clan as Mountain Shoshone also points toward one of the other commonly held opinions about them: that they were primarily on foot (and utilized dogs and travois), in contrast to the Plains Indians, who rode horseback across greater distances.

Horses came to North America via the Spanish explorers, so this method of categorization only takes us to the 1600s. Square this with the fact that a net made of twisted juniper bark, about 150 feet long and 6 feet high, was found in the nearby Absaroka Mountains. The size of the net and the wide weave

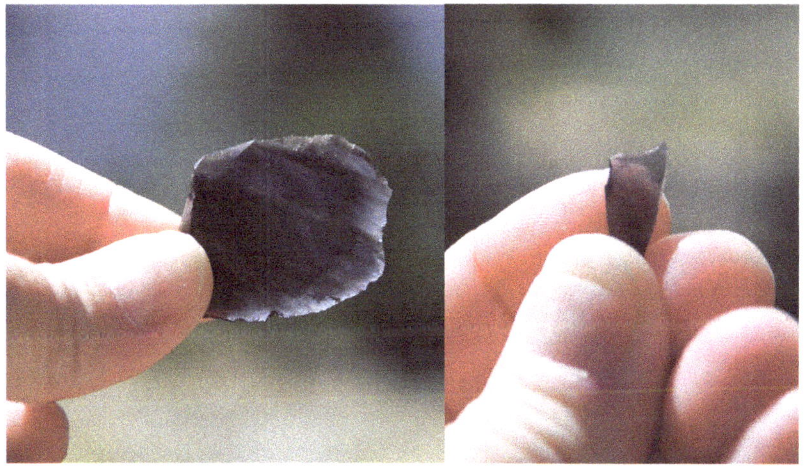

Fabricated knife blades found in Whiskey Basin. "Of all the Indian tribes, the Sheep Eaters were the most advanced in cultural things. Their bows were sought after all over the Western Hemisphere. Black obsidian points and other tools from Wyoming have been found as far as the Arctic Circle, and the Plains Indians had sheephorn bows from this area."

suggests that it was used to snag large game—likely bighorn sheep. It is dated to 8,800 years ago. Even today, Whiskey Basin hosts 1,200 bighorn sheep, the largest population of bighorn sheep in the world. It's no wonder the name Sheep Eater has stuck, even in the face of mitigating evidence.

Taylor asserts that the Mountain Shoshone/Sheep Eaters moved with the game, dwelling in the high altitudes of the mountains in the summer, and retreating to the valley in the winter. So the petroglyphs were likely pecked into the rock in the winter. What does this suggest about the artists who created them?

It's hard to imagine that a population who was struggling to gather enough food would take the time to painstakingly peck designs into rocks. Does this suggest that the petroglyph artists were prosperous? "The explanations from experts on what they mean lack proof," Taylor simply states.

Speculation is nonetheless irresistible. Theories range from the fanciful to the mind-numbingly mundane. Some suggest that the petroglyphs serve as No Trespassing signs for other clans, with the petroglyphs depicting the gods that protect the land. Some say they depict alien visitors. Some chalk them up to straightforward artistic expression. Theories hold that the petroglyphs depict stylized pictures of the tribe itself. Others suggest that the rock drawings illustrate sacred myths.

Stephen V. Banks a Dubois historian with ties to the contemporary Native Americans on the Wind River Reservation, cites the legends of the Shoshone about a Water Ghost Woman. "There are a lot of stories about the Water Ghost Woman and her helpers," says Banks. "The rays you see coming out of the figures in some of the petroglyphs could signify magical or mystical powers. The canyon is also a great place for a vision quest. In some of the petroglyphs, you'll see a hand, face, or leg right up against a crack in the rock—and the legend is that the cracks signify access to the 'Little People.' Often, on a vision quest, the seeker would suffer deprivation to the point of hallucination. They would believe that the little people took them through a crack in the rock where the supplicant would have his vision. After the ceremony was over, they led the seeker back out. But, if you talk to six different Shoshone down there on the reservation, you may get six different answers on what the petroglyphs mean and how a vision quest goes."

The archaeologist Lawrence Loendorf describes what a vision quest for the Crow meant. He writes that a young man would walk into lands such as Torrey Canyon, forsaking food, water, and fire for as long as four days, inducing hallucinations.

"If the supplicant were fortunate, he received a visit from a guardian spirit. This visit might begin with a 'little person' appearing to him while he was in trance. The little person would act as a go-between who led the man on a journey into another world where he would be introduced to the supernatural spiritual forces. There he would receive his power, perhaps from an eagle, a bison, or a bear. He would also be taught a medicine song and told to construct a bundle to hold talismans or sacred objects that were to be brought forth when he needed to call upon his spirit helper."

The artistic contributions of the Paleolithic people in the Wind River Mountains were not limited to petroglyphs. Soapstone bowls that likely originated in the

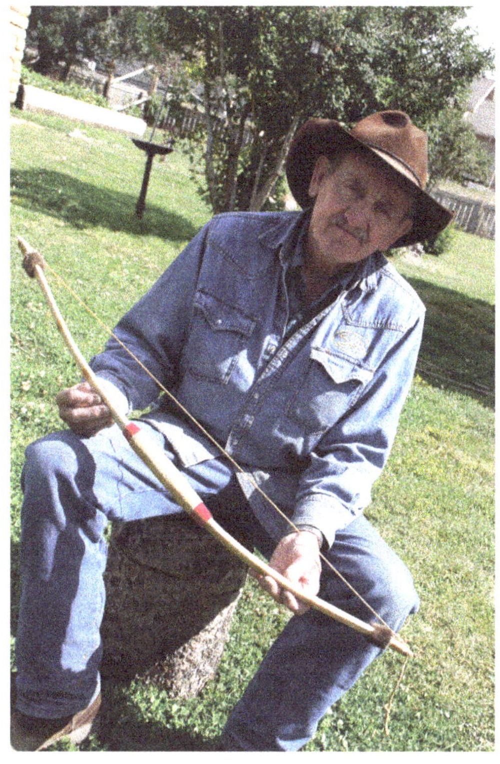

Tom Lucas with a sheep horn bow, which he makes in the old way. Historically the bows were made in the Winds by Native Americans and made their way as far south as Texas. Their reputation spread widely across the continent, and the Winds served as the crossroads of trade that disseminated them.

Winds have been found hundreds of miles away, and sheephorn bows were valued by other Native American tribes as far away as Texas. The sheephorn bows made by people in the Winds were short bows fashioned from the soaked and straightened horns of big horn sheep, scraped to form flattened sticks and bound with sinew. They could be crafted for tremendous bow strength, and they were light. Tom Lucas is one of very few people living today who can make a sheephorn bow using traditional materials and techniques. "It takes 10 to 15 days in water to soften the horns up," says

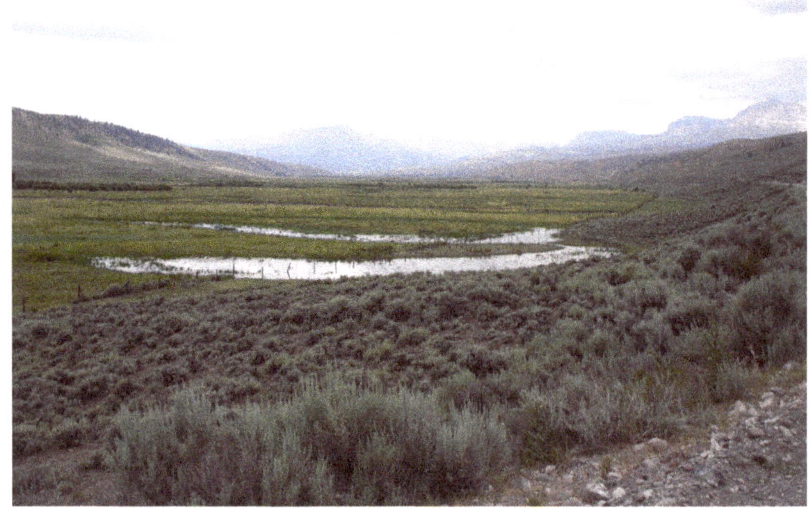

The flats where the DuNoir Creek drains into the Wind River at the river's northern end.

Lucas. "While they are wet, you lash them to a board. Then it takes longer than that—a whole lot longer—for them to dry. If you take them off too soon, they will curl right back up. Then you bind two of the pieces in the middle of the bow with sinew you save from your meat, and use hide glue to put it all together. You can't buy these materials; you have to find them in nature." Lucas has made 50 of these sheephorn bows over the years, and it takes him months to make each.

The craft and culture of Native Americans in the Wind River Mountains and adjacent valleys were spread far and wide. The Sheep Eaters are often considered an insular tribe, but this can be misleading. And Hollywood clouds the picture as well. Because of Western movies and early dime novels, the West, and "Indians," are rooted in the minds of many as dark-skinned men armed with rifles on horseback, with feathered headdresses and face paint. This is but a sliver of Native American history, one that starts in the 1600s and dies out in the late 1800s. The Shoshone have roots in the Winds going back at least 9,000 years.

Because they didn't ride horses, aggressively trade, make war, and eat buffalo like the Plains Indians, whites assumed that the Mountain Shoshone were relatively impoverished. "Of all the Indian tribes, the Sheep Eaters were the most advanced in cultural things," counters Banks. " Their bows were sought after all over the Western Hemisphere. Black obsidian points and other tools from Wyoming have been found as far as the Arctic Circle, and the Plains Indians had sheephorn bows from this area."

The river valleys that run on either side of the Wind River Mountains, draining water from the Continental Divide, end in fertile land to the southeast. But in the northwestern valley, the Wind River Valley, there's a place up closer to the river's headwaters that marks an ancient crossroads for migrating animals and the indigenous people. The South Pass is famous because of its role in the Oregon Trail, a path so heavily used by

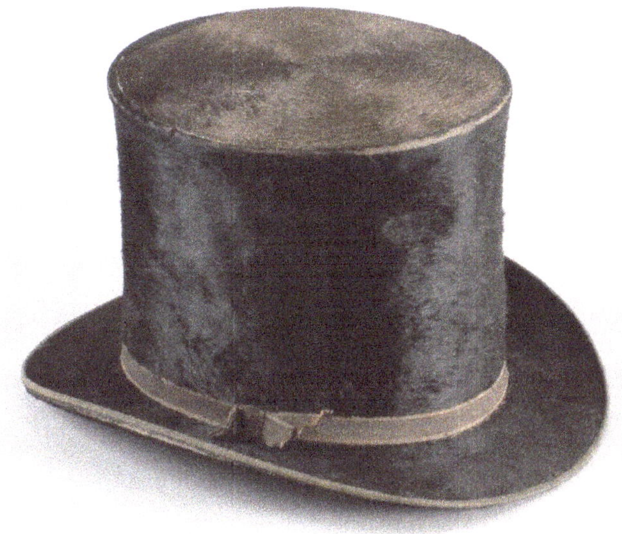

A top hat made from beaver felt.

white settlers that wagon wheels ground wide ruts in the rock, but it's the confluence of Union Pass and the Wind River Valley that mark the most notable intersection.

Two ancient Native American trails cross there to form a nearly perfect X, a fact noted and propagated by Stephen V. Banks. It's here where several geographical features come together. It's here where Dunoir (Du Noir) Creek drains down from the Absarokas to the north, and pours into the Wind River, which has its headwaters further northwest, near Togwotee Pass. It's here where Union Pass begins it journey over the Wind River

Mountains. Union Pass is a navigable—if somewhat treacherous—pass over the Continental Divide, and Dunoir Creek is the bottom of Dunoir Valley, a wide and hospitable path to and through the Absarokas. Various tribes, including the Crow and Shoshone, traveled east-west through the Wind River Valley, and north-south along Dunoir Creek and over Union Pass to the Green River Valley. Here is where the trading of goods extended the impact of the early people of the Wind River Mountains.

Here also is where the fur traders, mountain men, and Native Americans gathered for their yearly Rendezvous. These events, which attracted as many as 3,000 people, were generally centered in the Green River Valley, but the trails and trade routes of the Dubois crossroads were crucial for logistics. People poured through the passes and followed the creeks and rivers to level land conducive to temporary structures and easy visiting— and most importantly, plenty of good land for grazing.

What fueled this big gathering in a land that's still one of the most sparsely populated in the country? Beaver pelts.

"Beaver skin was the key factor that opened the western movement in the Western United States," Banks asserts. Mostly, the beaver pelts were made into hats. It took about three beaver pelts to make a hat, and the process was painstaking. In fact, the process is almost unbelievable. The guard hairs had to be plucked from the pelt, then the softer fur underneath was shaved off. The resulting fluff was placed on a tin table, and a bow with a taut wire was plucked in the center of the table, with the bow held vertically,

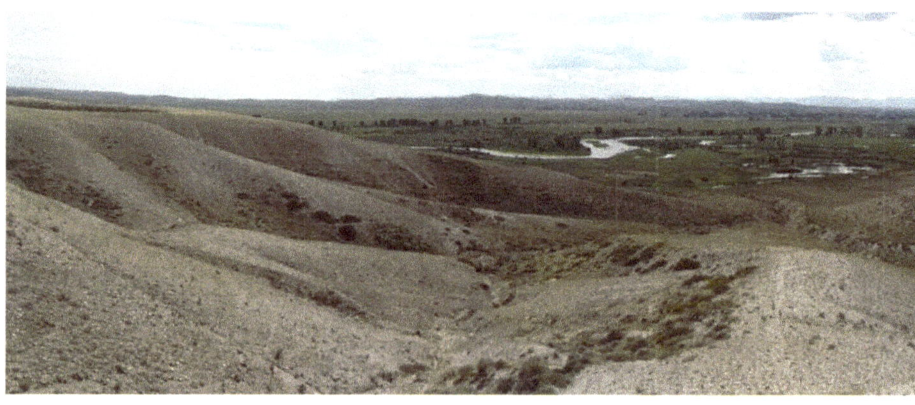

The Green River Valley, site of the 1837 Rendezvous. Trappers from Canada and the Pacific Northwest gradually joined trappers from the East to form the legendary mountain men of the Rockies. Their heyday was brief; by 1842 the fur trade had

perpendicular to the table. The hairs would vibrate and align in the same direction. They were then soaked in a solution that included cinnabar or its derivative, mercury, and pressed into disks. These disks were steamed and formed into hats. The hats were then dyed and brushed, and accents were added, like a hatband. One beaver fur hat would cost a year's wages for a sailor, according to diaries kept by the crew of Samuel Champlain. The hats were considered heirlooms that were passed down for generations. Beaver pelts were nicknamed "furry bank notes," and were the currency of the mountain men of the Rockies.

The mountain men bought supplies with pelts. For example, Banks says a pound of black powder would cost a mountain man three beaver pelts. A flintlock rifle would set you back 22 beaver pelts. A 1-lb bar of lead, which could make 18 round bullets, cost one pelt. In today's dollars, a pelt was worth $25. A typical pelt was a bit over a pound. Trappers preferred to hunt for beaver in late winter and early spring, when the beavers had their heavy winter coat.

According to local legend, beaver pelts were responsible for the arrival of the first white men in the upper Wind River Valley. François and Louis-Joseph de La Vérendrye came to the Dubois area in 1742 in search of pelts. The brothers were Canadian, exploring southwest from Manitoba. Trappers from Canada and the Pacific Northwest gradually joined trappers from the East to form the legendary mountain men of the Rockies. Their heyday was brief; by 1842 the fur trade had become much less lucrative. But while the craze for beaver fur was at its height, the Rendezvous became the event of

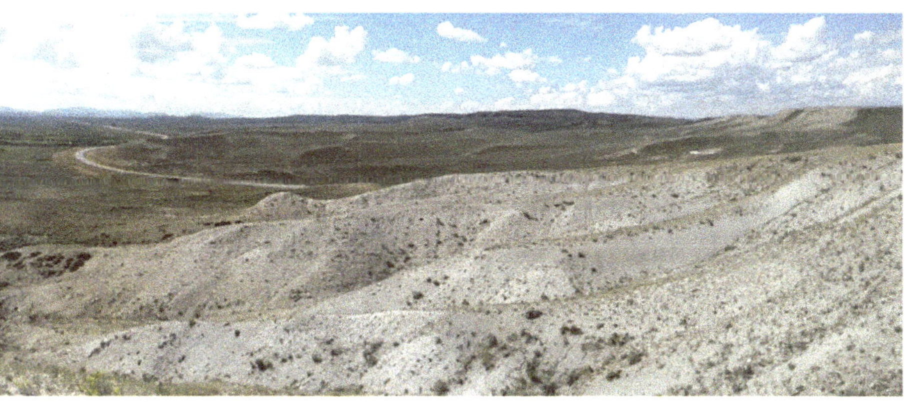

become much less lucrative. But while the craze for beaver fur was at its height, the Rendezvous became the event of the year in the West.

the year in the West.

The Rendezvous of the fur trappers were held from 1825 to 1840 in various locations. One of the earliest chroniclers of the Rendezvous was Alfred Jacob Miller (1810-1874), a youngish artist from Baltimore who accompanied the Scottish nobleman Sir William Drummond Stewart on an 1837 expedition based out of St. Louis. Miller was immediately struck by the landscape in Wyoming around the Winds. "I speak candidly & truthistically when I say…it's a new and wider field both for the poet & painter, for if you can weave such beautiful garlands with the simplest flowers of Nature—what a subject her wild sons of the West present, intermixed with their legendary history," Miller wrote in a letter to his friend Brantz Mayer on April 23, 1837. He painted several views of the 1837 Rendezvous in the Green River Valley, on the southwest side of the Wind River Mountains—both on location and for years afterward, back home on the East Coast.

Stewart may have been the aristocrat, but he was tough and disciplined, especially compared to his personal traveling artist. Marvin C. Ross writes in his book *The West of Alfred Jacob Miller,* "Quickly establishing his working routine on the trail, Miller realized that the most dramatic scenes usually occurred near sunup and sundown. He often left with the hunters in the morning and sketched until almost dark. He was permitted to employ someone to stand his guard duty and put up and take down his tent, but he had to combine his drawing with retrieving and picketing his horse and other trail duties. Dissatisfied with these chores because they occurred when the camp was most active—and when he needed to be sketching—he responded to Stewart's complaint that he was not doing enough pictures, by erupting, 'If I had half a dozen pair of hands, it should have been done!' Calmly, Stewart replied, 'That would be a great misfortune.' Miller could not resist asking why. 'It would be very expensive in the manner of kid gloves,' the captain continued. To his private journal, Miller confided that he had a rejoinder to his captain 15 minutes later, but 'too late.' Unfortunately, he did not record the riposte for our enlightenment."

The explorers and the mountain men were crossing the backcountry of the Winds and the other ranges of the Rocky Mountains, but they had help. "Their chances of survival would have been almost none if they hadn't associated with the Native Americans," says Banks. "They did not see Indians as the enemy."

Echoes Peter H. Hassrick, director emeritus of the Buffalo Bill Center of the West, in Cody, Wyoming: "Even at the time of the Lander Expedition in 1859 it was a mutual admiration society with the Shoshone. If you read the journals of the Lander Expedition, you see that the relationship is very positive between the Native Americans and the whites. The tribes back East, such as the Pawnee, pegged the whites for what they were and what they represented early on, and there was trouble, but as the expeditions went further west, that was not how the whites were seen."

By 1843 the Oregon Trail was being used by settlers moving east, rather than the trappers who had been trading along a path stretching clear to Vancouver, and north to the Hudson Bay. The fur trade was yielding to farmers. By the turn of the century, the Old West that lives in stereotype was gone. "…so rapidly was the West transformed from unknown Indian country into a settled region that artists had little time to prepare their pictorial record," writes John C. Ewers in his book *Artists of the Old West.*

Next came surveyors, engineers, and government. Exploration yielded to expansion of land claims. Married couples were granted 640 acres in "Oregon Country" for free, provided they farm it. Unmarried settlers were allotted 320 acres. [Oregon Country as late as 1853 extended eastward to the Continental Divide in Wyoming.] Frederick William Lander, an engineer and a general in the Union Army in the Civil War, laid down Lander Road, which skirted the southern end of the Wind River Mountains at South Pass and continued westward to Fort Hall, in Idaho. The sweep of white settlers across this challenging terrain was on.

His surveying trip in 1859 included a Dusseldorf artist named Albert Bierstadt (1830-1902) and Boston painter Francis Seth Frost (1825-1902). Alfred Jacob Miller painted stunning scenes of the Wind River Mountains, but Bierstadt was the artist who presented the sublime beauty of the Winds in a grandiose and romantic fashion that made a mark on the public consciousness.

Bierstadt seemed to have a personal agenda while painting his experience of the Rockies, from the Wind River Mountains and on up and northwest through Yellowstone. His epic paintings suggest that he felt he had something to prove. The United States was still a young country. Correspondingly, the American art scene was still beholden to the European art scene. Young American artists aspired to study in Europe from masters—or at the very least, tour the countryside, sketching and painting the architecture, ruins, mountains, quaint villages, and general culture of Europe. Bierstadt traveled to Germany as a young man, his artistic skills still quite raw, and over one summer, churned out such a body of plein air sketches that he returned from his sojourn in the Westphalian countryside in autumn with the chops to create stronger paintings—and the reference material to inform them. He was, in large part, a self-made man from a modest background, born in Germany but coming to New Bedford, Massachusetts with his family as a toddler. America was still growing and coming into its own. Bierstadt was too.

In painting large pieces depicting the Rockies, Bierstadt was making his own mark, and making a point about America's own majestic mountains. "If you read Bierstadt's letters, it's clear he was interested in the juxtaposition with the Alps," says Hassrick. "That was the context for the early painters such as Miller and Bierstadt. Miller painted many watercolors of the Native Americans he encountered. The visiting artists will write in their diaries that the painters who rush to Europe, who go to France and Italy and paint peasants, should come out here and paint the amazing, unspoiled, uncompromised people who are a genuine American subject. They were intent on making these people and the mountains symbols of America. It was a jingoistic slant on the American West."

On July 10, 1859, Bierstadt wrote a letter to the publication *The Crayon* from the road in the Rockies, in which he stated,

The mountains are very fine; as seen from the plains they resemble very much the Bernese Alps, one of the finest ranges of mountains in Europe, if not in the world. They are of a granite formation, the same as the Swiss mountains and their jagged summits, covered with snow and mingling with the clouds, present a scene which every lover of landscape would gaze upon with unqualified delight. As you approach them, the lower hills present themselves more or less clothed with a great variety of trees, among which may be found the cotton-wood, lining the river banks, the aspen, and several species of the fir and the pine, some of them being very beautiful. And such a charming grouping of rocks, so fine in color—more so than any I ever saw. Artists would be delighted with them—were it not for the tormenting swarms of mosquitoes. In the valleys, silvery streams abound, with mossy rocks and an abundance of that finny tribe that we all delight so much to catch, the trout. ... I have told you a little of the Wind River chain of mountains, as it is called....The mountains here are much higher than those at home, snow remaining on portions of them the whole season. The color of the mountains and of the plains, and, indeed, that of the entire country, reminds one of the color of Italy; in fact, we have here the Italy of American in a primitive condition.

The Winds—and all of the Greater Yellowstone area—were a dazzling sight for artists. But more often than you might think, the early drawings, prints, and paintings of the region were done without firsthand experience. The most notable example of this is the case of Thomas Moran (1837-1926). The England-born artist is well known for his images of Yellowstone, but at least some of his iconic paintings were done from photographs, secondhand reports, or the drawings of other artists. One of most prominent peaks in the Grand Tetons, Mount Moran, was never seen by the namesake artist. Moran played a large role in convincing congress to make Yellowstone a national park, but he never saw the dramatic eastern face of the Tetons. The Grand Tetons were formed by a buckling in the earth's crust, with one plate pushed up to reveal a sheer, ragged vertical plane, and a more gentle decline on the other side. The iconic, dramatic exposure of the Grand Tetons' east face is what is photographed, painted, and climbed by most people. [Incidentally, a similar situation occurs in the Wind River Mountains, with the southwestern side facing Pinedale showing the more dramatic face, and the Dubois side exhibiting a relatively gentler climb.]

This didn't stop Moran from painting both the Tetons and the Winds. Bierstadt's firsthand observations, too, are questioned in regard to his paintings of the Tetons. Although today it seems particularly disingenuous for an artist to paint something he or she has never seen, this wasn't the case

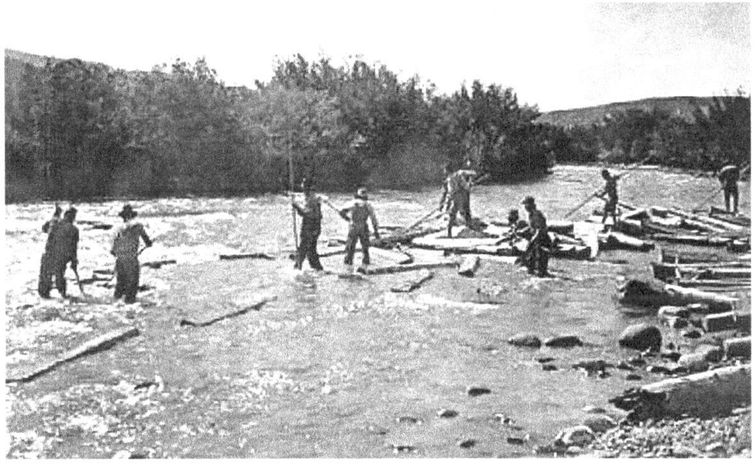

An infusion of a large contingent of burly Scandinavians arrived in the Winds, an immigrant society who worked as "tie hacks," roughing out railroad ties from cut timber in the mountains, and floating the lumber down the Wind River to Riverton.

in the past. Consider the particularly entertaining 1515 woodcut by Albrecht Dürer depicting a rhinoceros, complete with riveted armor and scaly legs. Likewise, in 1870, Moran received a commission from *Scribner's* magazine to illustrate an article on the Yellowstone. He completed the commission using written descriptions and very rough sketches done by explorers.

The transcontinental railroad was completed in 1869 when a golden spike was driven in Promontory Summit, in the Utah Territory, connecting the Southern Pacific with the Union Pacific railroads. The Oregon Trail saw its traffic decrease dramatically; the West was truly opened up by the trains. Cheyenne, and then Laramie, grew rapidly as the railroad was built across the southern edge of Wyoming. Paintings of Yellowstone served the purpose of the railroads, boosting ridership as Americans traveled to sightsee. And the railroad enabled Wyoming businesses to ship resources and products to distant markets. But the role of the Winds as a crossroads diminished… with the exception of the infusion of a large contingent of burly Scandinavians arriving in the Winds, an immigrant society who worked as "tie hacks," roughing out railroad ties from cut timber in the mountains, and

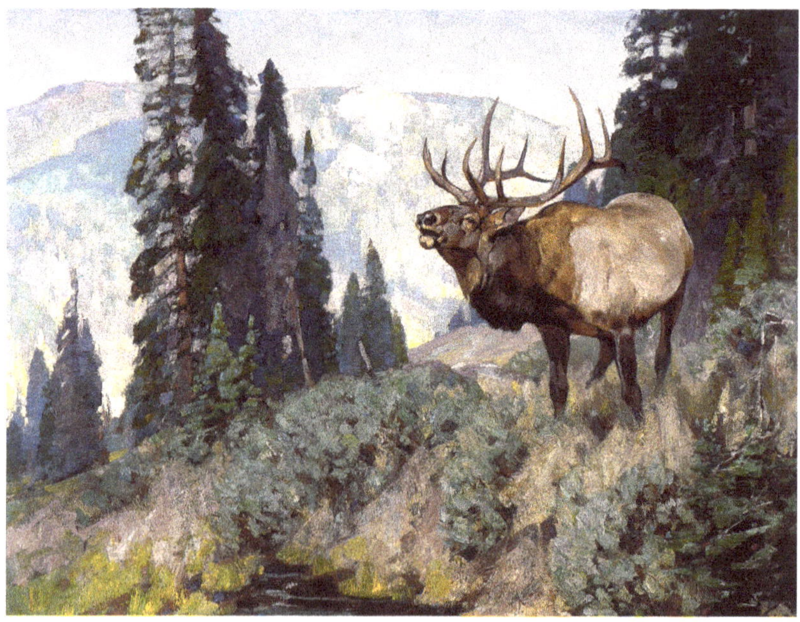

Berlin-born wildlife artist Carl Rungius was no soft-handed dilettante. He traveled deep into the Wind River Range backcountry to hunt and sketch, usually with an outfitter.

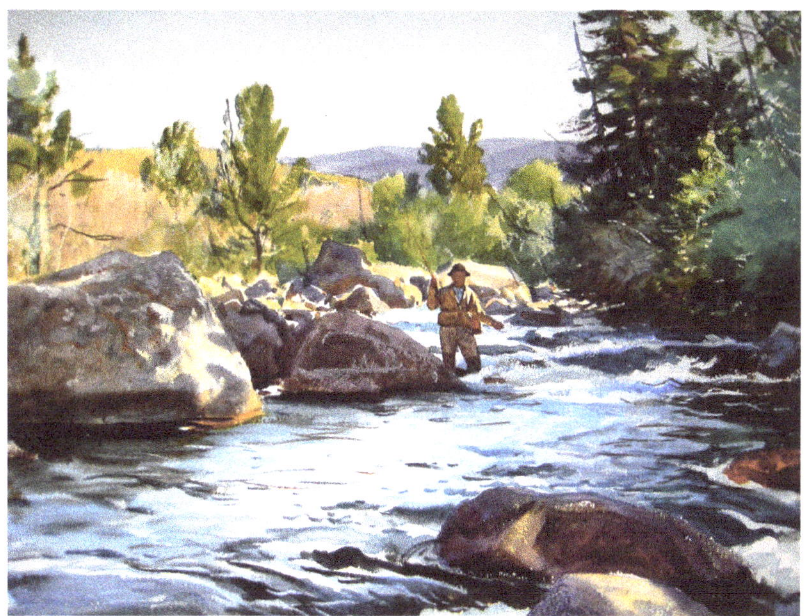

Ogden Pleissner, born in Brooklyn, spent his summers as a teenager in Dubois, attending a camp focused on hunting and fishing. The artistically minded kid also sketched western scenes and animals. Starting in the 1930s, Pleissner and his wife spent every summer for more than 12 years in Dubois.

floating the lumber down the Wind River to Riverton, where the ties were used by the Chicago and Northwestern railroads. An estimated 10 million railroad ties came out of the Dubois area, with the Wyoming Tie & Timber Company working out of its headquarters near Brooks Lake. The trees along the Wind River Mountains were cut with a two-man crosscut saw and the limbs stripped. The tie hacks could cut a tree into the right proportions for a railroad tie—seven inches thick and eight feet long—by eye. Each tie weighed about 150 pounds, green. In 1913, a tie hack would make 12 cents per tie. The trees were cut in winter, when it was easier to drag them across the snow-covered ground, and sent down the river as the spring thaw raised the waters.

About 12 miles west of Dubois, the Wyoming Tie & Timber Company erected a memorial in 1948 honoring the tie hacks. The bas relief sculpture depicts a tie hack wielding a broadaxe. The plaque reads: "Erected to perpetuate the memory of the hardy woods and river men who made and delivered the cross ties for the building and maintenance of the Chicago and

Northwestern railway in the Western country."

Cars and trucks would soon replace trains in many instances, and the railroad tie business died in the Wind River Valley. But another industry had caught hold in the meantime: Dude ranches.

The Dude Ranchers' Association traces its history back to 1886 and the Custer Trail Ranch, in the North Dakota Badlands. Theodore Roosevelt came out to the West and fell in love with the lifestyle, which blended hospitality with horseback riding and ranch work to invigorate mental and physical health. TR bought a ranch nearby in 1883, and dude ranches became trendy. By the 1920s, dude ranches had taken hold all across the West, from Montana to Arizona.

Trains made it easy to travel to Wyoming, and dude ranches offered an authentic experience and a soft bed. Into this situation rode two notable artists, Ogden Pleissner (1905-1983) and Carl Rungius (1869-1959). Rungius, widely regarded as a giant in wildlife art, spent a formative four months in 1895 on a ranch near Cora, Wyoming, a few miles outside of Pinedale. It was the young Berlin-born artist's first trip out

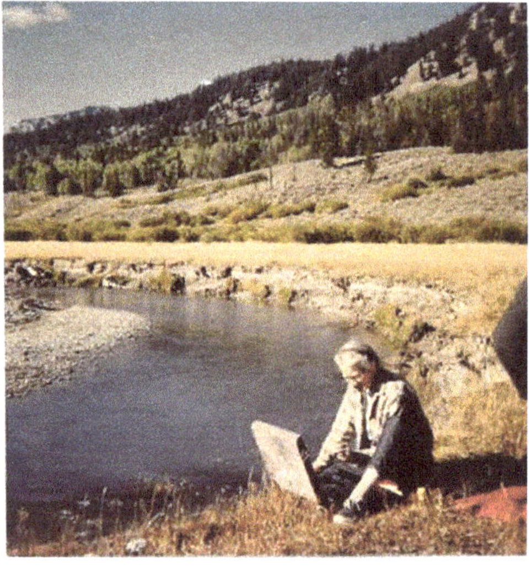

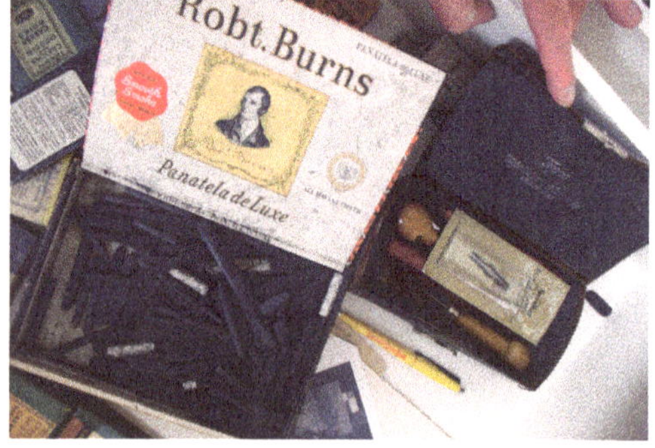

Two lesser known artists who emerged out of the dude ranch world had a greater impact on arts in the Wind River Valley: Mary and Joe Back. Top: Mary Back painting on location in the Wind River Mountains. Bottom: Back's materials, as preserved at Headwaters Arts & Conference Center, in Dubois.

west, and the beginning of a long career painting the Rockies in Wyoming, Montana, and Canada. He came to hunt with his uncle, and Rungius used the resulting trophies to sketch the big game of the Rockies. His stay in the Wind River area persuaded the artist to immigrate to the United States the following year.

Rungius was no soft-handed dilettante. He traveled deep into the Wind River Range backcountry to hunt and sketch, usually with an outfitter. Tales of his exploits abound, ranging from raiding Native American graves, to chasing the Sundance Kid as part of a posse, to having his broken leg set by a taxidermist. In later years he focused more on the Canadian Rockies, but for decades he spent winters in New York City, painting studio pieces based on his sketches, and passing the rest of the year in Wyoming.

Pleissner, in contrast, was born in Brooklyn, but he spent his summers as a teenager in Dubois, attending a camp focused on hunting and fishing. The artistically minded kid also sketched western scenes and animals. Starting in the 1930s, Pleissner and his wife spent every summer for more than 12 years in Dubois. An avid fisherman, Pleissner became known for his sportsman scenes, working in both watercolor and oil. His outdoor scenes were popular with magazine publishers. But in some circles, he was better known as a correspondent/war artist for *LIFE* magazine in World War II.

Two lesser known artists who emerged out of the dude ranch world had a greater impact on arts in the Wind River Valley: Mary and Joe Back. Joe was born in Ohio and came to Wyoming by way of California. Mary was born in Minneapolis, raised in Vermont, attended a rustic college in Kentucky, and arrived in Wyoming with Joe via Chicago. The crossroads of the Winds pulled in two more artists.

Mary and Joe Back took over the abandoned Lava Mountain Lodge, 20 miles west of Dubois on Highway 26 in 1935, and ran it for four years. They then bought a bigger dude ranch, the Rocker Y, and worked that enterprise until they moved to contribute to the war effort during World War II—Joe as a shipyard welder, and Mary as an aircraft mechanic in California. After the war, they were back in Wyoming, but they strayed from the dude ranch business. The couple had met at the Art Institute of Chicago, and both were keen to pursue their artistic interests. Joe worked as a game warden and a hunting guide to help make ends meet, and Mary began teaching art to interested parties in the Wind River Valley.

Mary Back was very encouraging to people in the Wind River Country who

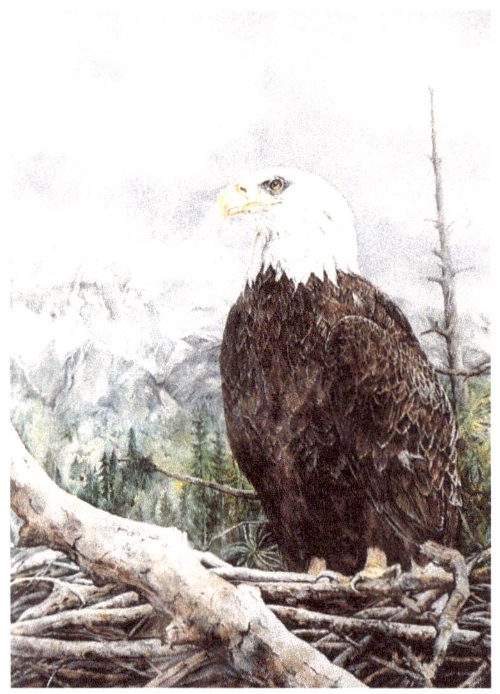

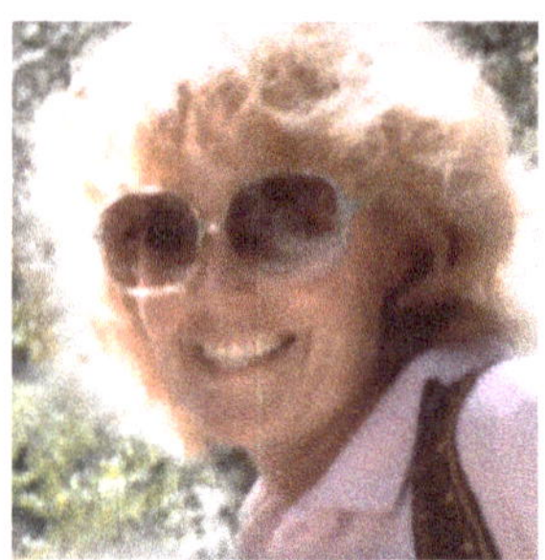

*Susan Kathleen Black
and two of her watercolors:
"Grand Teton Resident" and
"Moose on the Rocks."*

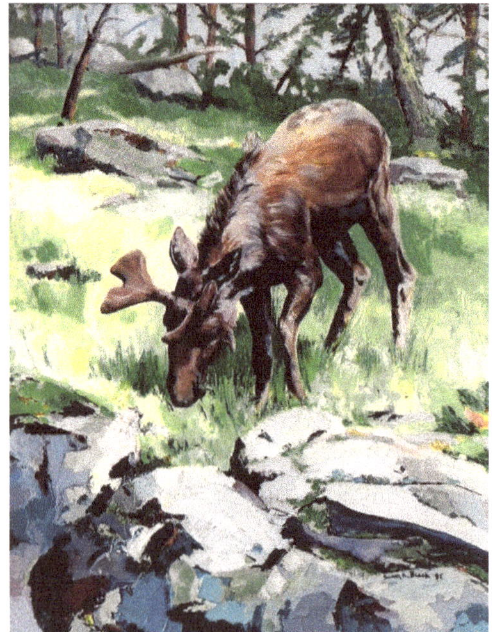

were interested in art. Such efforts produce two consequences: It creates more artists in the area and a more exciting arts scene, and it fosters an appreciation of art that can boost collecting. The extent of her reach via art education is incalculable, but her lessons may have been the lesser of Back's two major contributions to art in the Winds. In 1949, she and Joe founded the Wind River Valley Artists' Guild.

It started out modestly. The WRVAG hosted an annual show that hung in the local gymnasium, and the patron's dinner was held in the backroom of a saloon. But its popularity grew rapidly. By 1957, the show featured 340 pieces, drawing submissions from California to Kentucky, from Dunoir to Afghanistan. In the mid-1980s, Guild member Laney Hicks bought a concrete building on the Wind River at the west end of Dubois that once housed a wildlife museum. The WRVAG moved its annual show there, and local officials started making plans to build something more appropriate at the location. (The concrete building was deemed too drafty and rather ugly.) With money raised locally and with grants, the town of Dubois put together $1.4 million and built the Headwaters Art and Conference Center. With the opening of Headwaters in 1996, the northwest side of the Wind River Mountains had a municipal building devoted to visual art.

The facility was crucial in bringing the Susan Kathleen Black Foundation to Dubois.

Susan Kathleen Black was married to Jim Parkman, a Houston businessman who appreciated Black's interest in painting

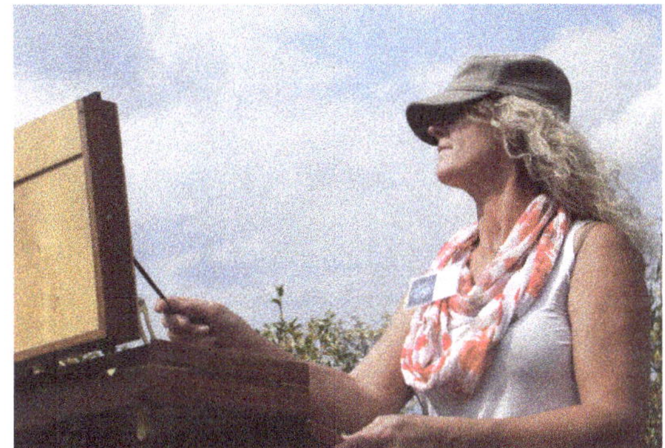

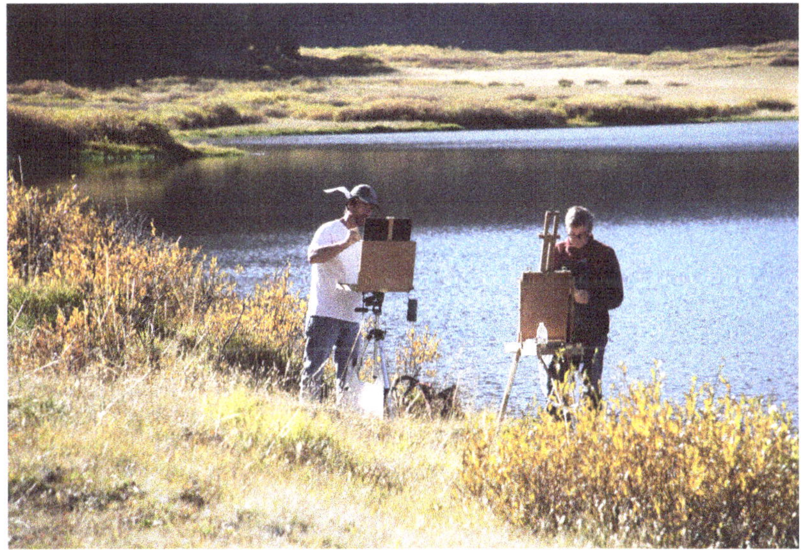

SKBers painting in the Dubois area.

and wildlife. When Black passed away, Parkman sought a way to honor her memory. Her love of the wild Rockies, and her gratitude for the art instruction she received in Big Timber, Montana, from Jessica Zemsky and Jack Hines, pointed in the direction of art education. But in what form, and where?

The Susan Kathleen Black Foundation was formed in 2001 (and incorporated as a non-profit in 2003), and the first SKB workshop—inspired by an idea from Pam Cable—was put into motion. SKB would host an event to allow artists to stretch their skills and hone their approach, the kind of event that Black loved to attend.

Cable answered the question of "what," and a sculptor/painter in Dubois supplied the "where." John Phelps served as a guide on a backcountry trip in the Winds attended by Lee Cable, Pam's artist husband. The trip nearly killed both of them, thanks to the vagaries of the wilderness, but Cable returned to Colorado with a love for the Wind River Mountains. When Phelps pointed out to the Cables that Dubois had the new Headwaters facility—a perfect venue for an artists' workshop--the pieces were in place.

After one workshop in Divide, Colorado, the annual SKB gathering made its home in Dubois in 2002. The weeklong event attracted some of the best wildlife artists in the country, along with developing wildlife artists

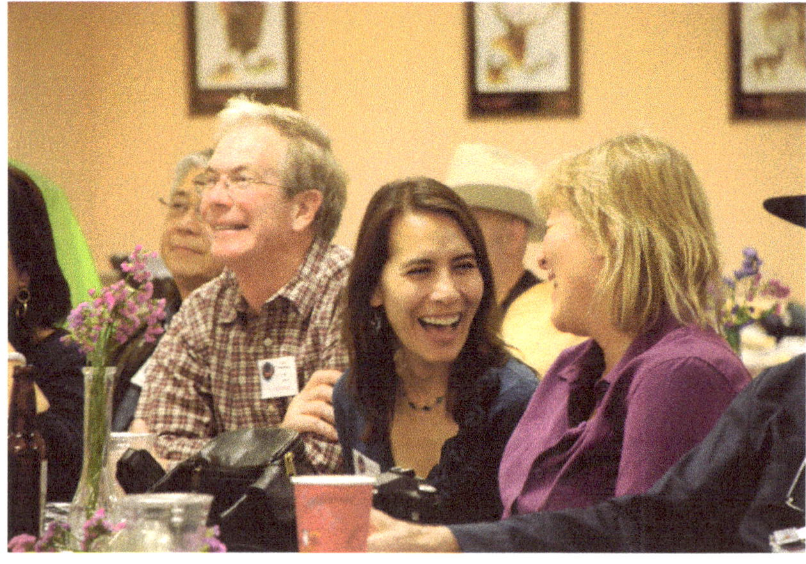

SKBers gather at Headwaters for food, laughter and lectures.

eager to learn in a collegial environment. The rugged beauty of the Wind River Valley quickly became part of the draw, and plein air painting grew as a major component of the SKB workshops. Luminaries such as Robert Bateman, John Ruthven, James Gurney, John Seerey-Lester, Greg Beecham, Stephen Quiller, Tom Lucas, Everett Raymond Kinstler, and Mort Solberg taught at SKB more than once over the years, and the event now regularly draws more than 100 artists. The level of the work has improved precipitously over the last several years.

And what is notable about the gathering is that it pulls people from Michigan and Louisiana, Australia and Ft. Collins, Florida and New York City, Canada and Great Britain. The crossroads continues to pull diverse people to Wind River Country.

Crossroads. Places of opportunity. A nexus, a place to make a decision. A place that promises fame, fortune, fate. A meeting place. Where differences blend. Where creation takes place. A spot that nurtures exploration, adventure, growth.

The Wind River Mountains provide a last barrier to the far west, create watersheds on both sides of the range, and offer wild nature and conditions that test a human's mettle. They funnel animals of all kinds—including the bipedal type that, in addition to enjoying hunting, fishing, and exploring, likes to create art—through a part of Wyoming that undeniably and inexplicably gets under a person's skin. Has anyone stayed in the Winds by accident? There's a common link through the ages, from prehistory to today, from the Clovis people who made their way from New Mexico to hunt in paleo-indian encampments in the high altitudes 11,000 years ago to the rich Easterners who sought space and fresh air in the dude ranches to the 100+ artists who descend upon Dubois for SKB each September. The Wind River Mountains have proven to be a notable artistic crossroads. The art can be as mysterious and totemic as any found elsewhere, with creatures embodying deep instinctual impulses, scenes and atmospheres that evoke a higher being, and grandeur that both celebrates human achievement and underlines humanity's relative insignificance.

Chapter 3

Spirits in the Cracks of Rocks

When was art first made in the Wind River Mountains, and by whom?

Considering that this question points us about 13,000 years into the past, it is impossible to answer it definitively. Archaeologists have confirmed the presence of Clovis points in the Wind River Mountains, supporting the theory of humans arriving in North America via the Bering Strait, even as a smaller group of others assert that the Native American tribes we know today migrated from Central and South America. Fasten your seat belts, because many so-called facts are questioned in this chapter.

The first question may be, what is Native American art?

Those outside of Native American culture here in the North America— call us Whites, the White Man, European Americans, colonizers, non-natives, whatever you like and what fits—can easily write a long list of examples of Native American art. It might start with obvious choices, such as pottery, paintings on bison (buffalo) hides, and extend to

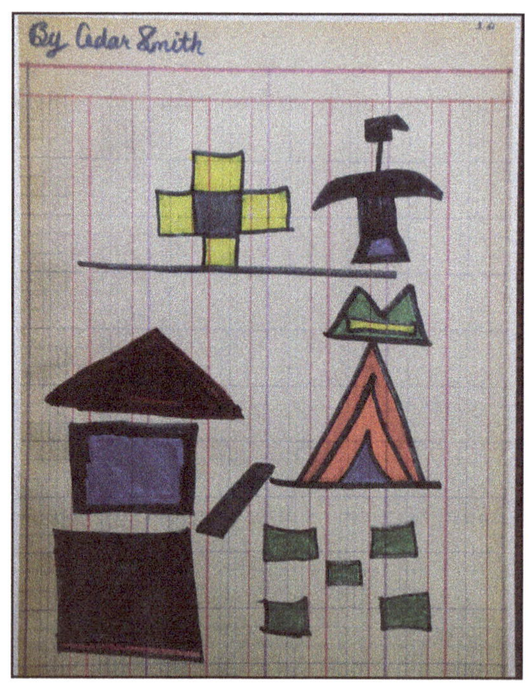

Traditional Native American symbols drawn by a student at the Wyoming Indian Middle School, in Ethete. The author saw a stack of photocopied and stapled handbooks of traditional symbols sitting on a table in the school's library—although he was told they were not for his eyes.

exquisitely beaded moccasins, or a ceremonial pipe, among many other items. And, that list would be both correct and missing the point.

Appreciating Native American art may require a different approach. One can examine it using scientific method or modern modes of art criticism, but the motivation behind the art's creation, which is rooted in Native American worldviews, is different enough from mainstream American culture as to render such approaches nearly irrelevant. To get in the right frame of mind to view Native American art, one must first accept that for many Native Americans, certain objects possess something approaching personhood. A ceremonial pipe has a presence. It is not special because of its exquisite workmanship. It is important as imbued with spirituality during creation. The symbology of Native American art varies from tribe to tribe, and much of it is obscured from non-native understanding—sometimes intentionally so.

The author saw a stack of photocopied and stapled handbooks, 8 ½" x 11", sitting on a table in the library of the Wyoming Indian Middle School, in Ethete. Near the front of this booklet were several pages of common symbols from the tribes on the Wind River Reservation. It was like a key or codex that could potentially unlock some of the symbology found on area rock art, clothing, and sacred objects. I hadn't looked at it for more than 10 seconds before the booklet was closed to my eyes. I was told the book was not for me.

One figure, one concept that shows up in several forms of Native American art, especially the petroglyphs and pictographs, is that of Water Ghost Woman. Who is she and what does she represent? This knowledge is not for non-natives. "We run into the situation that most bands, clans, or tribes have their version of the legends of Water Ghost Woman. They are intermingled," one elder told me. [Native American sources will not be identified in this book because in the past, Indians who shared their knowledge outside the tribe were treated badly by those who feel the culture is in constant danger of being appropriated and rendered unsacred.] Water Ghost Woman was mentioned by several others, and yet, when one knowledgeable Native American source was asked about her, the source feigned complete ignorance of such a thing.

And yet, the student of Native American culture, if patient, somehow gleans the meaning of such figures and legends. Water is viewed in an unusual way among the tribes on the Wind River Reservation. Some believe the Water Ghost Woman pulls kids underwater and cuts their heads off. One teacher on the reservation pointed out that it would be very unusual to see kids flipping water bottles the way much of America's youth currently does for fun. The primary reason is that you don't play with water on the rez—you respect it. "Water is central to our lives and our ceremonies, that's why we respect it," explains one source. "Most people don't know about the Water Woman story, but they do know they don't play with water because of water's place in their everyday lives." Water Ghost Woman is often described or pictured with a turtle, and while you likely won't get an explanation for this, patient listening to elders and other members of the tribe starts to fill in some of the blanks. Turtles symbolized the ability to move between worlds—water and land, earth and spirit world. Through a growing knowledge of the symbols, some petroglyphs start to suggest meanings.

But even if an elder could be found who would be willing to interpret all of the imagery on the rocks, clothing, and sacred objects of the tribe, chances are another elder would interpret it all differently.

In one of the Indiana Jones films, the hero's quest is to find the Holy Grail, the chalice from which Jesus drank, according to legend. Jones finally finds himself in the room that houses the Grail, but there are many chalices,

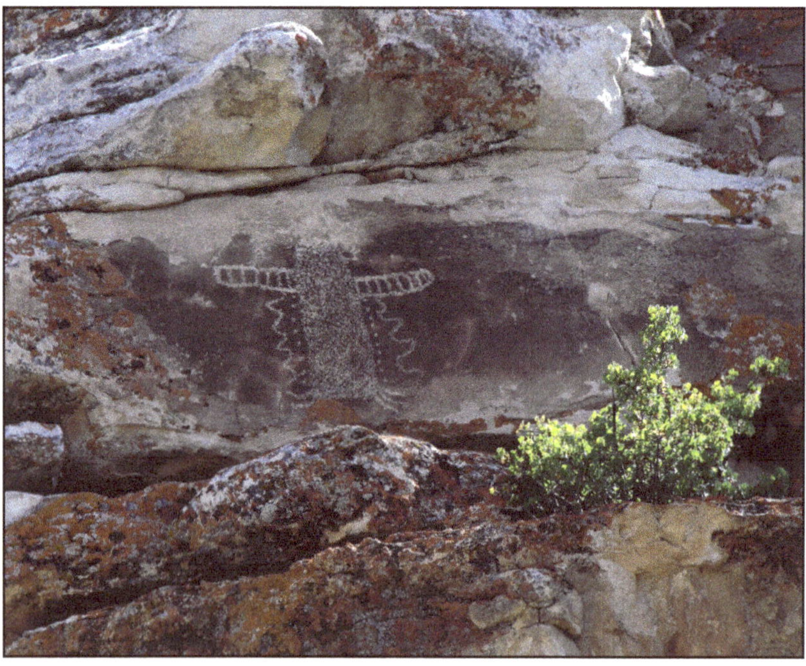

one more ornate and beautiful than the next. But the most modest chalice is the one the carpenter's son used, according to the movie. Likewise, sacredness is not bestowed on an object in Native American culture because it is beautifully crafted. Its provenance makes it sacred. It was used by a chief or medicine man in ceremonies; the honor it is given comes in part by the deeds and character of its user. The object becomes sacred; it is not necessarily made that way.

In contrast, most art in the Western/European World gains its value from the painting or object's inherent beauty, and via the reputation of its maker. Outsiders have a difficult time not viewing Native American art through this familiar lens. Additionally, although some Native American art is pictorial and seems to be intended as a way of communicating ideas, many pieces of Native American art are valued by the tribes for their role in tribal life—not just their utility, but their power to command respect. And beyond the beauty of simply well-crafted functional items of everyday life, Native Americans in the Wind River Mountains have utilized hides to make teepees, parfleches (envelope-like backpack/bags), and shield covers…and, of course, rocks as surfaces upon which to draw and paint.

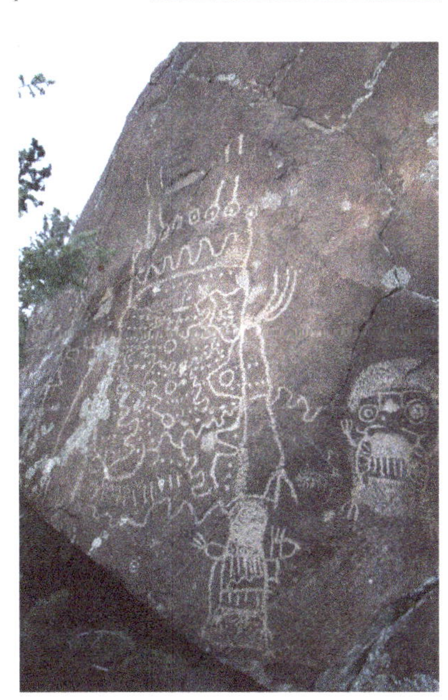

The purpose of ornamenting rocks and cliffs seems slightly different than art made on hides. The hides usually tell stories, often in a circular or spiral-shaped series of images. These painted images are often put into the category of Winter Counts. Each object or image depicted represents an event of note for that year. It could be a comet, a smallpox breakout, or a

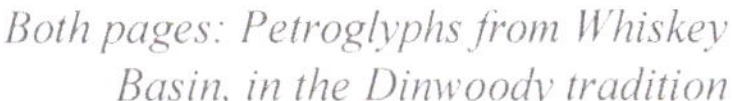

Both pages: Petroglyphs from Whiskey Basin, in the Dinwoody tradition

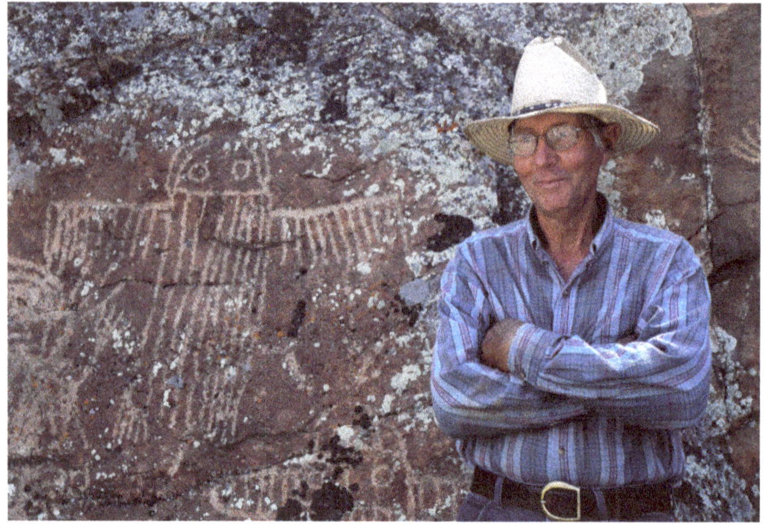

Local historian Tory Taylor by a petroglyph on Ring Lake Ranch.

similarly significant event. The Winter Counts represent years and years. They depict battles, hunts, courting, spiritual events, and situations in which an individual got him- or herself into trouble. The parfleches have symbols that reflect the tribe and the purpose of the bag. And the rocks?

Perhaps the most honest and scientific response to that last question comes from Tory Taylor, a Dubois area historian, naturalist, and hunting guide. "I don't know," says Taylor. "And until I get my time machine and dial it back to when they were made, and stand beside the artist and ask, 'What are you doing?', I won't be satisfied."

We are left with educated guesses, once again based on what the Shoshone and Arapaho share and what those studying Native American culture and history have figured out. Unlocking the secrets of the petroglyphs requires approaching Shoshone and Arapaho culture holistically. If one takes the time to understand the importance of the golden eagle in Native American tradition, for example, then the depiction of a "thunderbird" on the erratic boulders of Whiskey Basin makes a little more sense.

Rock art created by earlier tribes date back at least 3,000 years, but even that rough measure is challenged by some experts. Lawrence L. Loendorf favors the cation-ratio dating technique, which examines the number of positive ions detected in the "varnish" into which the petroglyphs are inscribed, both in the inscribed lines and in the "untouched" varnish around the pecked out lines. Loendorf acknowledges the limitations of this dating method. And while Loendorf is respected—nearly revered—within the scientific community and among laypeople with a scientific bent in regard to Wyoming's petroglyphs, it is quite easy to find those who disagree with many of Loendorf's hypotheses…especially in the Dubois area. Assertions in Loendorf and Julie E. Francis's book *Ancient Visions: Petroglyphs and Pictographs of the Wind River and Bighorn Country, Wyoming and Montana* get challenged by members of the Shoshone and laypeople in the area.

We can all agree that the Sheep Eaters were the ones doing the carving, though, right?

No. We can say they were one of the groups who created petroglyphs, with some confidence. The Shoshone lived in the Great Basin, west of the Winds, from about the year 1000 to around 1200, when a great drought drove them north and east. By 1500 the Shoshone were utilizing the Great Plains, as well as the Rockies. The Shoshone's neighbors on the Wind River Reservation, the Arapaho, utilized territory in South Dakota in the late 1700s and arrived in Wyoming as residents when the

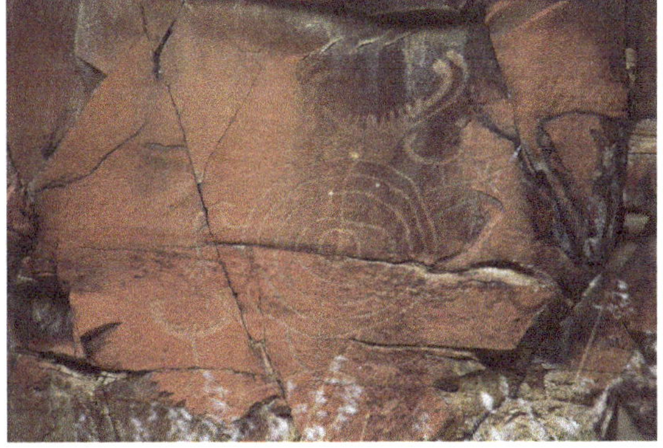

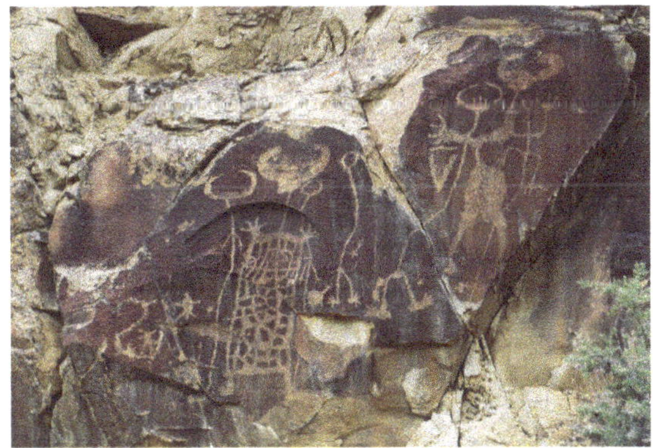

Petroglyphs on Legend Rock.

reservation era began. The Arapaho were displaced by the creeping presence of white settlers, put on the move, variously taking stands and acceding land to the settlers. In 1864 the Southern Arapaho were living along Sand Creek in Colorado with some Cheyenne when whites slaughtered as many as 500 Native Americans, including a sizable number of women and children. The Northern Arapaho moved into the southern part of Wyoming, eventually petitioning the U.S. Army to let them stay on the Shoshone reservation in the Wind River Valley. Shoshone chief Washakie agreed to let his former enemies stay on the reservation.

The Shoshone lived throughout the Rocky Mountains, and they also hunted on the Plains. They were the first Native American tribe in the area to get horses (from the Spanish) in 1700, which greatly expanded their range. At some point a group of Shoshone focused most of their time on the Rocky Mountains, including the Wind River chain. They and the Crow inhabited what is now Yellowstone National Park, until the government's creation of the United States' first national park made it illegal to live, hunt, or even collect medicinal plants there. (Native Americans still need to get special permission from the government to hunt and gather medicinal and dietary plants in Yellowstone, a traditional hunting ground for them.) In the Whiskey Basin area, east of Dubois, the Mountain Shoshone lived in the valley in the winter and high in the mountains

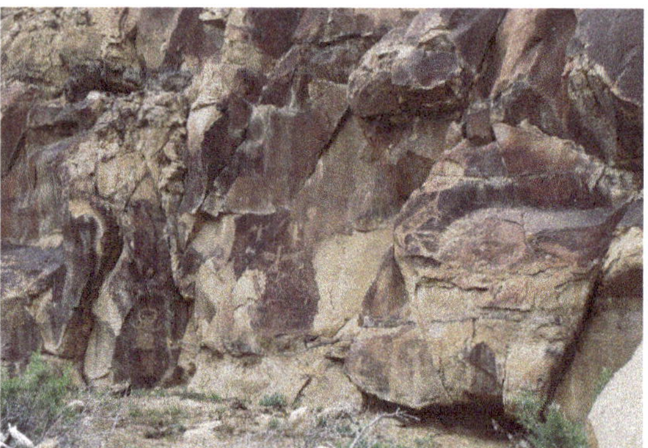

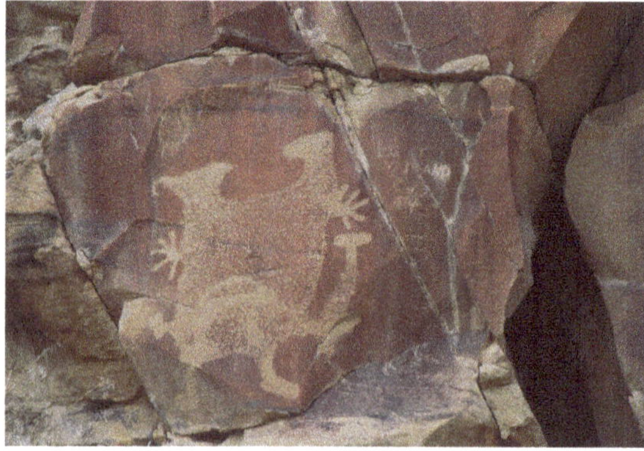

Petroglyphs on Legend Rock

in the summer. Other tribes called these Mountain Shoshone "Sheep Eaters," and they undoubtedly ate bighorn sheep—along with all the other traditional foods that other tribes ate. Traces of pine nuts, goosegrass seeds, chokecherry, and other plants and grinding tools confirm this. Nevertheless, in general, tribes were given names by other tribes based on what they were perceived to have eaten, where they preferred to live, and how they otherwise conducted themselves. These names were often misleading, and sometimes derogatory. The Shoshone were known as the Snake for years. The Crow even now resist the name Crow, in some circles. The Mountain Shoshone never only or even primarily ate sheep. (Tribes of all kinds usually just called themselves "the people" in their native tongue.)

We're not even sure that it was the Mountain Shoshone who picked up stone tools and pecked out the petroglyphs. The dating of the varnish suggests Shoshone, but this is still a hypothesis. Here's why.

The tools varied, from "choppers" to "abraders" to "hammerstones," and Loendorf believes that sometimes the images were pecked directly, and sometimes indirectly, as with a hammer and chisel. The varnish or patina on the rocks is a combination of clay minerals from the environment and oxidation, with the rock underneath showing very white when pecked. Individual artistic processes show that some figures were deeply inscribed and others lightly abraded. Archaeologists use the subject matter to help determine the age of the petroglyphs. For example, a horse-like form suggests that a petroglyph was pecked after 1700, while a bow and arrow indicate a drawing no older than 1,500 years.

If the inhabitants of the Wind River Mountains who pecked out the petroglyphs were making this art 3,000 years ago, then labeling the artists as Shoshone becomes questionable, if for no other reasons than the distinction between tribes clouds with age, and the divisions of the indigenous people 3,000 years ago didn't fit modern categories. But if these people—whatever we call them—followed the seasonal pattern that the Mountain Shoshone did, then it is logical to assume that the petroglyphs that face the three lakes leading to Torrey Canyon were manufactured in summer. Our culture may want to think of the making of these images as leisure activity.

"The creation of the petroglyphs was undoubtedly deliberate or meaningful," asserts Taylor. "The Crow will remind us that culture (and art) is one of the stepping stones of humankind evolution. Making tools was a milestone, learning about fire was a milestone. And spiritual beliefs set us apart from other critters. It's all there in our DNA. Art is common in

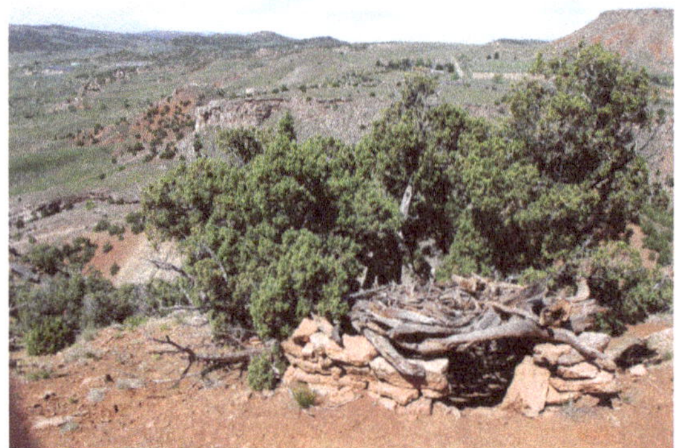

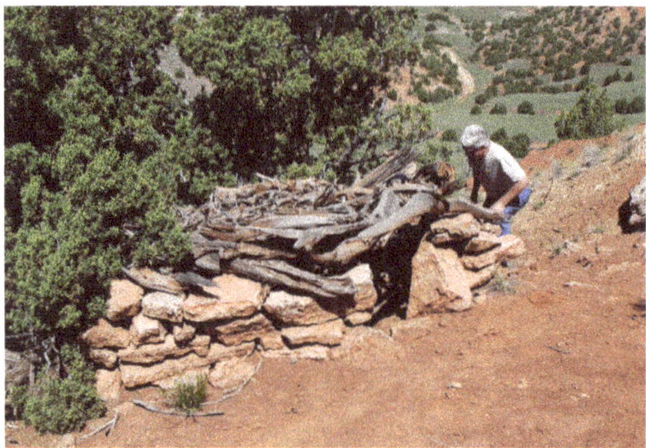

An eagle trap discovered outside of Thermopolis. Native Americans would hide under the low structure, attracting eagles with a dead rabbit on a stick. When an eagle landed, the man would grab the legs of the eagle and pluck three feathers before releasing the raptor.

cultures all over the world. These folks did this for a reason. It's clearly not idle doodling. They weren't going to waste time or calories like that."

Then what were these petroglyphs for?

"Maybe they were marking their territory," Stephen V. Banks offers. "Some think [Torrey] canyon is sacred enough that these were meant to serve as 'No Trespassing' signs. Maybe the images mean, 'You will be under these people's spell and you will never get out of here if you come further.' But the places where petroglyphs are found are also great places for a vision quest."

Some rock art seems to depict hunting scenes, with elk bugling, deer running, rabbits sitting, antelope loping. Scenes depicting horses and bows and arrows make non-native minds further imagine hunts. But while there are plenty of people who will espouse this view, a closer look at the concept of a vision quest offers a wider answer.

Vision quests are a rite of manhood for several tribes. Fasting, isolation, prayer/meditation—or, a hallucinogen such as peyote, if the person were a member of the Native American Church—give the young man dreams and waking dreams. The young man is seeking "medicine," a power or force to protect him and provide him with a role in the tribe. He may be "visited" by Coyote, or Wolf, or some other spirit taking an animal shape. What he sees, hears, or learns would suggest what his job may be in his clan. He may get an indication that he should be a medicine man, or a warrior, for example.

However.

Accounts of vision quests are as indeterminate and elliptical as anything else in Native American culture. Some say the young men would stand in front of a petroglyph until a vision arrived. Others say the petroglyphs are the records those on vision quests left for others to see and interpret. If their vision included a buffalo, they incised the image of a buffalo on a naturally varnished rock face. The very name "vision quest" is not standard within tribes. "We aren't seeking a 'vision' per se when we participate in that ceremony," says one source. "We are looking for help, spiritual and possibly physical, for either ourselves or a loved one."

Petroglyphs in the Dinwoody tradition (the style of petroglyphs found from the Wind River Valley to Thermopolis) do not all face the same compass direction, nor do they appear on only one kind of rock. But they do all face water, which seems significant. At the Buffalo Bill Center of the West, archaeologist Bonnie Smith is examining the relationship between petroglyphs of thunderbirds and remains of golden eagle nests. She is finding a correlation, although she is also finding vision quest/fasting shelters near eagle nests as well, and eagle traps. Eagle traps, eagle nests, vision quest shelters, thunderbird petroglyphs, water—they are often close by.

An eagle trap is a small structure made of stones and branches that obscure a brave soul who holds a dead rabbit on a forked stick through the top of the trap. When a golden eagle lands to eat the rabbit,

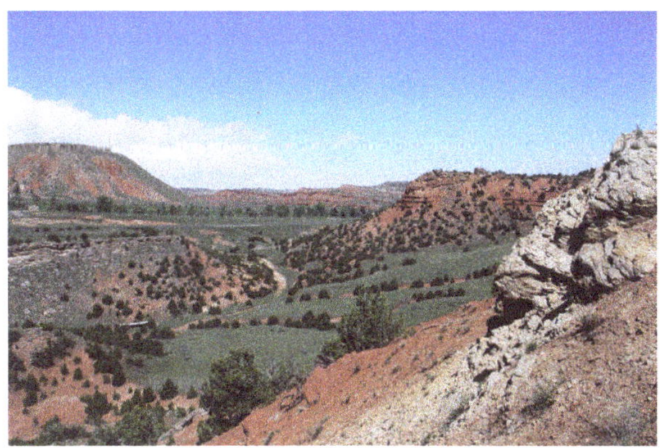

View from the eagle trap.

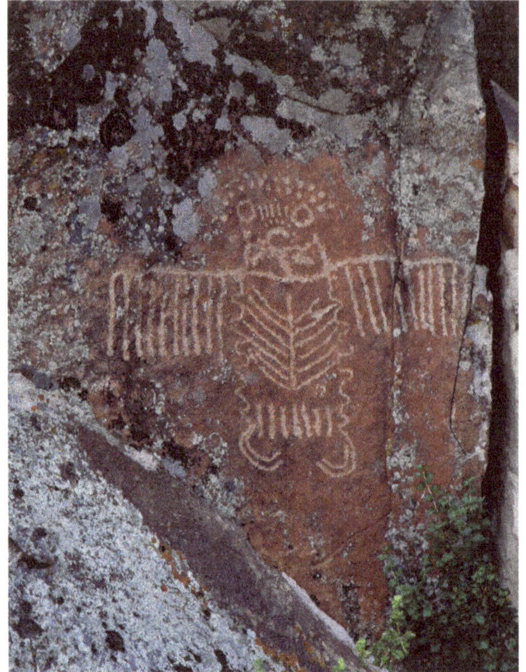

Petroglyph of a thunderbird.

the human grabs the legs of the eagle, plucks three large feathers (two from the tail, and one primary feather from the wing), then sets the golden eagle free. Obtaining feathers this way is a great honor, and the feathers are used for ceremonial objects and headdresses. The Shoshone and Arapaho hold family to be most important, and this extends to grandparents, aunts and uncles, and ancestors. The possession of golden eagle feathers was a symbol of earned honor and achievement.

Legends say that the cracks in the rocks are the doorways between the spirit world and our world. Through these cracks, the Little People would come into our world and make mischief. (If you want to drive an archaeologist crazy, ask them if the Little People are real.) Occasionally, the petroglyphs are situated to reinforce the idea that some of the anthropomorphic (human-like) and zoomorphic (animal-like) figures are of the spiritual world, seemingly emerging from the cracks in the rock.

Some petroglyphs look more humanoid than others. In general, an upright stance and the presence of arms and legs designate an anthropomorphic drawing. But there is great variation within anthropomorphic petroglyphs. Some have another being in the belly area, suggesting a pregnant woman. Some have hats or headdresses. Dots drip down vertically from the outstretched arms of some figures, which is often interpreted to depict rain or hail. Some have pronounced phalluses. A few in Whiskey Basin have thin lines emanating from the figure, and sometimes these lines lead to other, smaller figures. Is this a family tree? Or a depiction of how a god is tied to, and influences, humans?

Bonnie Smith reminds us that the "oddness" of these images is "similar to some of the images and sculpture we see from the Maya, Olmec, and Aztecs. These folks were having religious experiences, and many felt they were changing form into something 'else.' These are figures in transformation, we see it culturally over and over, universally. Peyote has similar mind-altering effects of fasting. They were trying to transform."

It's easy to view some of the anthropomorphic petroglyphs as looking like space aliens, if not creatures from the spirit world. Accordingly, some observers (but no scientists that we encountered) wonder if they do in fact depict visiting aliens. The reality is that many petroglyphs look "alien" to non-natives, but the legends and traditions of the Shoshone are rich enough with intriguing imagery without having to add extraterrestrials to the mix.

Back to Earth. The creators of the petroglyphs may comprise two groups of people, a group of Uto-Aztecan and later Numic-speaking people who lived thousands of years ago, and the Eastern Shoshone who inhabited Wyoming and beyond, hundreds of years ago. One petroglyph at Legend Rock, a cliff one city-block long located 23 miles outside of Thermopolis with an amazing and extensive collection of petroglyphs, is thought to depict Lodge Boy, a mythic figure of the Crow (and other tribes). So were the Crow or a proto-Crow tribe

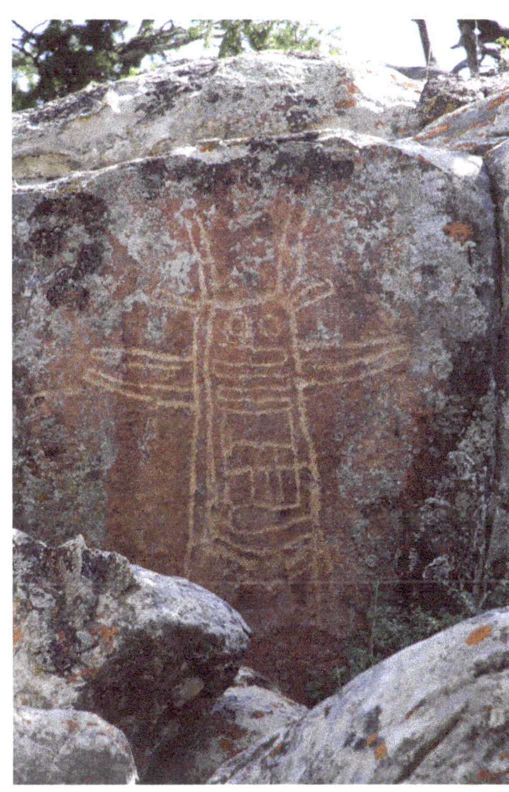

An anthropomorphic petroglyph.

pecking some of these petroglyphs?

Native Americans, going back to Pre-History, moved around—but not
without reason. They weren't nomadic. Calling their movements yearly
migrations doesn't quite do the job either. There is evidence that in the
Winds, people moved slowly up the mountains in spring and summer
as various plants reached their peak of edibility and availability. The
same goes for game, as the rams move up higher in the mountains in the
spring, for example. When they needed something, they traveled to get
it, purposefully. "Current migration research coming out of the Wyoming
Migration Initiative shows that migratory ungulates such as mule deer, elk,
and pronghorn, follow a 'greening,' which is part of their migration and one
of the factors leading to the choice of these ancient migration corridors,"
Smith says. "So if early people followed the animals, they are following
a migration." Tribes crossed over into other tribes' territories, sometimes
resulting in disputes, sometimes tolerated.

Long-distance trade has thrived in North America since at least the year
1000. "Even the Clovis people, dating back 13,000 years or more, were not
unstructured people, like a pack of wolves flowing across the land," says
Taylor. "Stone tools show they went to the same places time after time,
traveling great distances. These folks knew exactly where things were--
where to get a certain stone, where to trade. They had a knowledge of the
land and they knew where they wanted to be at a certain time of the year.
They knew the whole region, not just where they lived. In later centuries,
but before Wyoming was settled, some items coming from the Spanish in
New Mexico made it to Montana within two weeks. These folks moved
around a lot. They knew a big country."

Pipestone from Minnesota, black obsidian from Yellowstone's Obsidian
Cliff area for projectile points and knives, cowrie shells from the Pacific or
further afield—Native Americans in what we consider the isolated area of
the Wind River Valley had a wide trading network. Sheep horn bows made
in the Winds made their way as far south as Texas, and had a reputation
spread widely across the continent. The Winds served as their crossroads of
trade.

The precise shifts in where tribes lived over the centuries are not well
documented. And how exactly the Mountain Shoshone came to live in
the mountains is debated. An official publication from the Wind River
Reservation asserts, "It is probable that the Sheep Eaters of Yellowstone
Park were stragglers of the Northern Shoshones driven into and forced

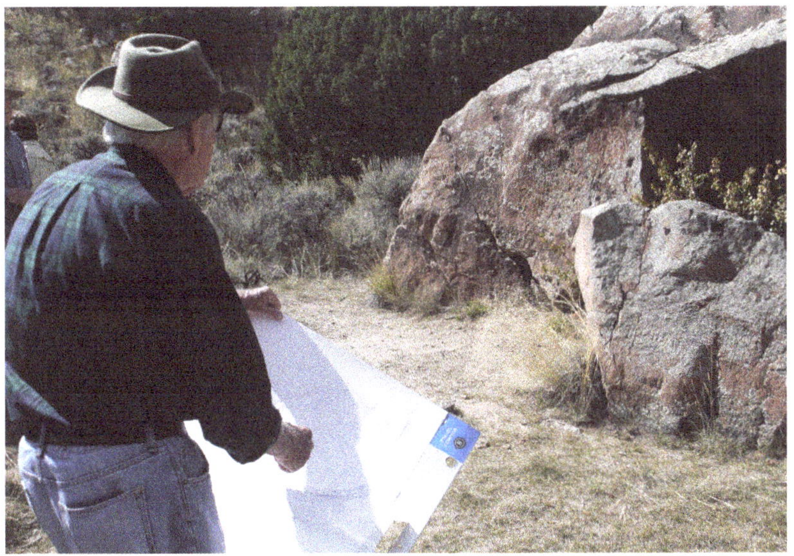

SKB artist John Ruthven sketching a petroglyph.

to live in the high mountains by their enemies," states *The Wind River Reservation Yesterday and Today: The Legends—The Land—The People.* "The last of the Sheep Eaters left the park as late as 1879, then joined neighboring tribes and lost their identity. Togwotee, namesake of Togwotee Pass, a mountain pass located in the high Wind River Mountains, was one of these people. He was one of the last independent Sheep Eaters. A feared medicine man, a trusted guide and a subchief under the famed Chief Washakie, he was a man of many accomplishments."

The source goes on to assert that the Shoshone were not a warlike tribe and their enemies acquired firearms before they did. They used dogs for packing and for watching their horses. They did not live like Plains Indians. "They used snowshoes and could run and jump between cliffs with these," it says. "It was a hard life in the mountains. They did not like to dance or anything like that, they just looked for food. They were clean people."

Meanwhile, historians and archaeologists strongly insist that the Mountain Shoshone, and the Eastern Shoshone in general, were Plains Indians. The Shoshone pushed north into Canada only to have the Blackfoot tribe run them back down to what is now the Canadian border, and further south into Montana and Wyoming. Spanish horses made their way up through the tribes from the deep Southwest at about the year 1700, with the Shoshone then the Crow becoming much more mobile with their arrival. The Crow

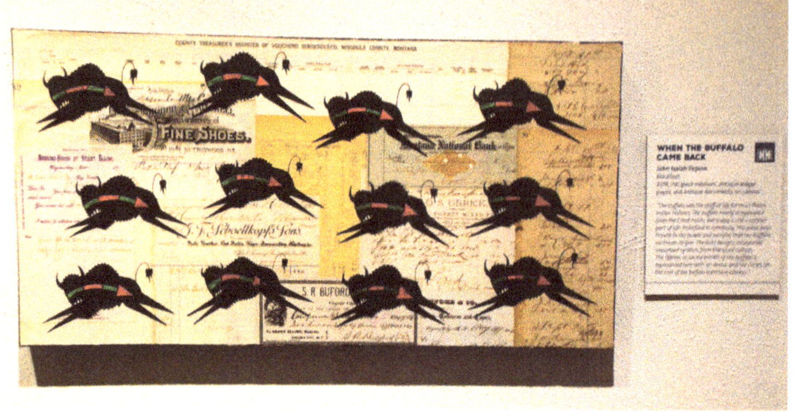

*"When the Buffalo Came Back," by John Isaiah Pepion.
A modern take on ledger art.*

were present in the Yellowstone area by 1800, the time when significant contact with French trappers marked the beginning of the influence of white civilization in the Winds. The Shoshone were then known as the Snake tribe, especially among those using propaganda to justify poor treatment of the Native Americans. "Furtive, wretched and misshapen creatures were

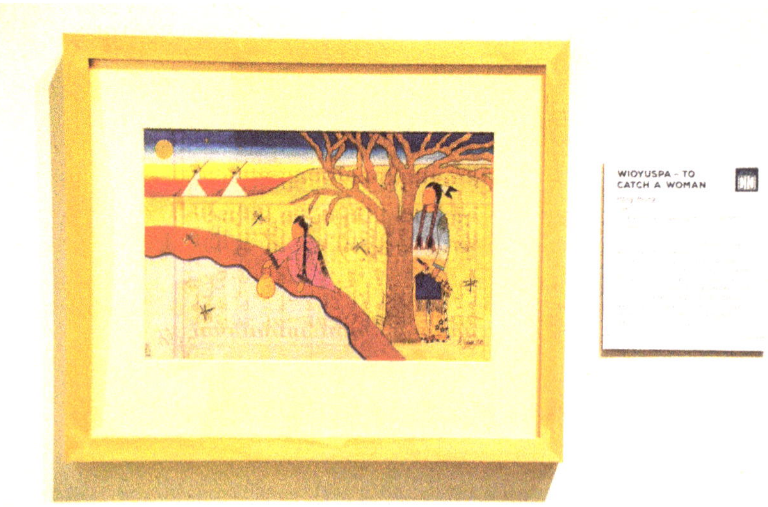

*"Wioyuspa—To Catch a Woman," by Holly Young.
A modern take on ledger art.*

also described by [early explorer Charles] Le Raye, with the explanation that they were called Snakes because they customarily lived in caves and had to be dragged out to be exterminated like reptiles," Burton Harris wrote in his 1993 book *John Colter: His Years in the Rockies*. A much earlier source not only echoes this negative view, but espouses it. E. S. Topping refers to the Mountain Shoshone as "refugees from the Shoshone and Bannock tribes" "as timid as the animal from which they derive their name"…"they are small of stature, and in brain diminutive, and compare unfavorably with

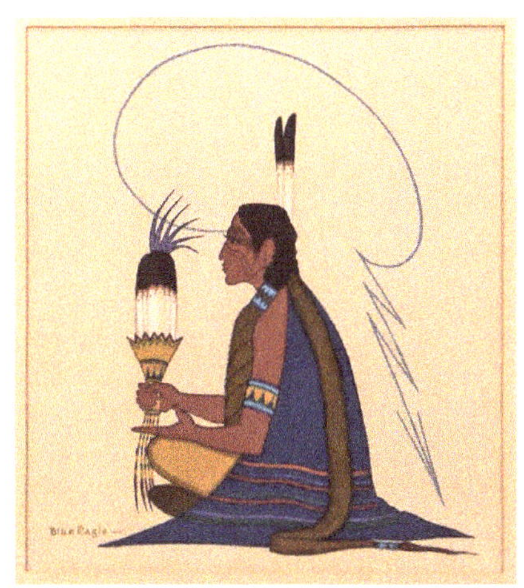

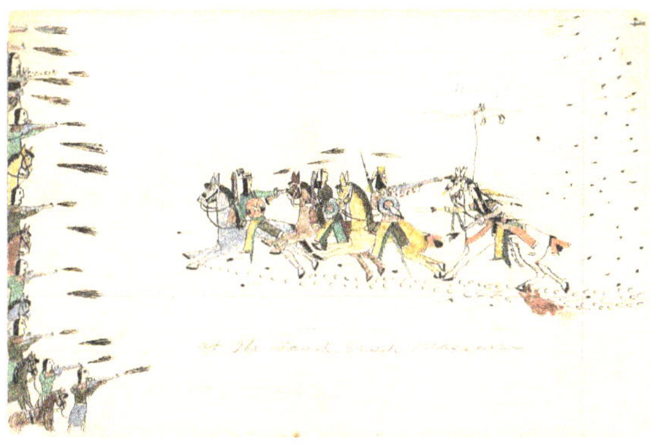

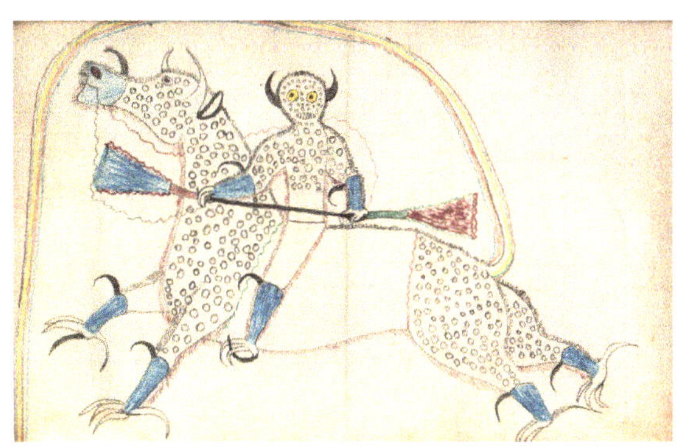

Top: "Man with Peyote Fan," by Acee Blue Eagle (1909-1959), a Creek/ Pawnee artist.

Middle: "At the Sand Creek Massacre," by Howling Wolf (1849-1927), a Cheyenne artist who was present at the massacre.

Bottom: Dream or vision of himself changed to a Destroyer and riding a Buffalo Eagle, by Black Hawk (ca. 1832-1890), a Lakota artist .

their relatives, the Shoshone." Topping also refers to them as "impudent" and needing to be "subdued."

Stephen V. Banks paints a more accurate picture. "Of all the Indian tribes that the early trapper Osborne Russell (circa 1840) had anything to do with, the Sheep Eaters were the most advanced in cultural things," says Banks. "They by far produced the best quality of tanned hides. They were more of a loner type group—not the dumb grubbers or diggers of the Great Basin as some suggest. They stayed in small family groups because they knew how large a group could be to survive. They were less warlike than other local tribes; they were good warriors but they didn't fight unless they had to."

The culture clash was on. In the beginning, the whites from the east were more cordial toward the Native Americans, arguably only because they couldn't survive in the Winds without their help. If tribes didn't have a reason to fight the trappers and explorers, then they welcomed them with considerable hospitality. A middle ground was spirited trade of goods. Before the arrival of whites, the beads the tribes used to ornament their clothes and other objects were large and often hand-carved. Whites brought uniformly made, smaller beads—and more importantly, muskets, powder, and musket balls—plus other tools and fabrics that were considered desirable. But as Strothers Burt wrote, "No two races whose psychologies are so different as those of the Indian and the white man find each other in crises. I knew an old lady down in Arizona who shuddered every time an owl hooted because that was the signal-cry of Geronimo and his warriors."

A Shoshone elder shared the tale of a white man and a Native American man who met on the prairie and exchanged gifts as a sign of friendship. The white man gave the Native American a valuable coin. The Native American gave the white a good rock, smooth and the perfect shape for crafting into a number of useful tools. They smiled and thanked one another, and as they were walking away, each threw their new gift on the prairie. Once they both realized what had happened, the white man went over and picked up the coin and put it into his pocket, and the Native American picked up the discarded rock and put it in his pouch, and they parted ways. Their worlds were so different, any understanding took considerable wisdom and patience.

Additionally, tribes across the continent appreciated the coyote as a trickster, and Native Americans were not above tricking the white people. Remember that the tribes got horses from Coronado. And why did Coronado cross the Rio Grande in 1541? Not merely to get to the other side.

He was chasing gold. An Indian slave known as "The Turk" told Coronado that there was a vast city of gold just further north, cajoling Coronado into central Kansas—where The Turk wished to go. Some speculate that part of The Turk's design was to lure Coronado and his priests and soldiers deep enough in North America to ensure their death.

Similarly, in 1934, John E. Underwood, the editor of the *Dubois Frontier*, asserted that, "In the summer the Indians wandered down from the upper reaches of Wind River, with tales of terrible winters that ravaged the upper country. Tremendous winds, impassable snows, bitter cold—these were the substance of the stories they told. Yet every fall the Indians drifted again to Upper Wind River, singly and in families, their ponies loaded down with supplies; pack horses carrying luxuries and necessities; heavily laden travois dragging behind horses and even behind the long-legged dogs that were a part of every Indian entourage. There came a day when a white man happened by chance to accompany the Indians for a winter in the upper country, his keen brain pondering the anomaly of the Indian tales and their annual disappearance into the mountain, so he lands up the river, investigating for himself. The truth then appeared. The upper country, sheltered in some mysterious way by the mountains, had less snow, less cold, possibly as much wind, as the bleak wastes about Fort Washakie. As the wily Indians had

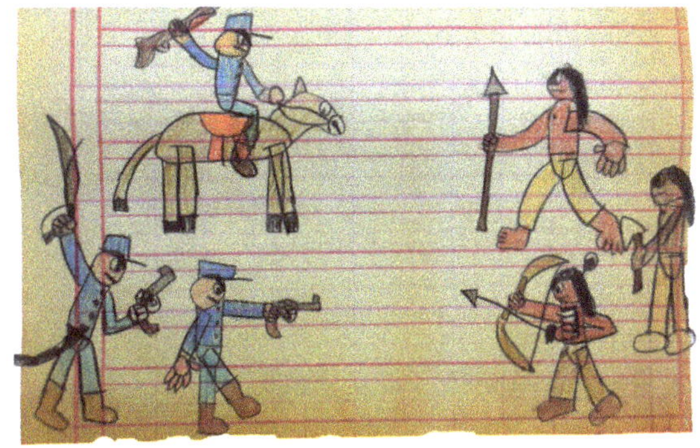

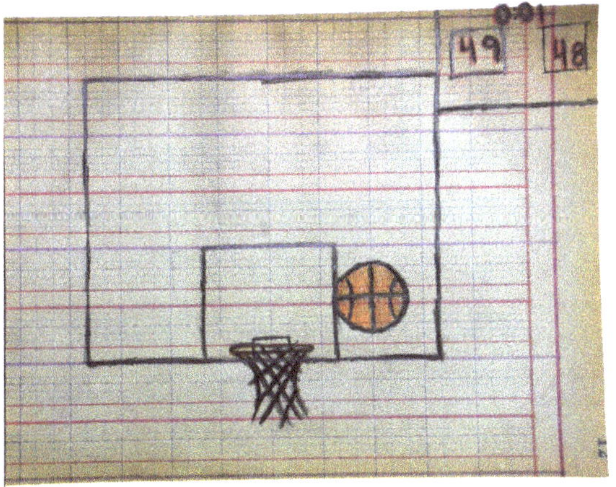

Two drawings done in 2018 by children at the Wyoming Indian Middle School, in Ethete.

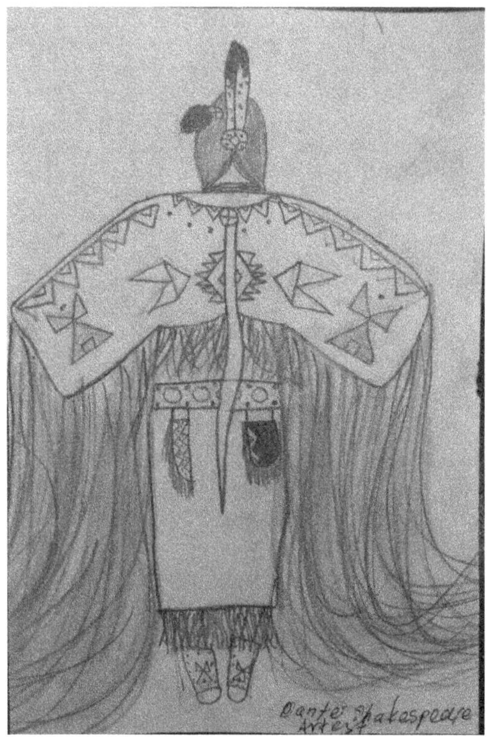

*Sketch for a dress by a student at the Wyoming
Indian Middle School, in Ethete.*

foreseen, following that discovery, it was only inevitable that certain hardy frontiersmen, reaching out for a new land in which to live, moved into the upper country."

The tribes were soon outnumbered by the settlers and soldiers pouring in to Wyoming. Armed resistance on behalf of the Native Americans, while possibly honorable, was fruitless, just postponing the inevitable. Tribal leaders realized this, and the craftiest of them, Washakie foremost among them, made alliances with powerful white men. Washakie was more than just pragmatic and open to whites—he befriended them.

When the government was offering help, Washakie made sure his Shoshone got their share. At the peak of government help, they received annual support in the form of blankets, overcoats, shirts, stockings "and much else," according to historian D. B. Shimkin. In addition, four times a month, each lodge received "a quarter of beef. The first week a dwelling would receive a front quarter, and the following week it would be issued a hind quarter," according to R. B. David. "Besides the meat, each Indian received a regular soldier's ration of two pounds of bacon, rice, beans, baking-powder, coffee and sugar, as well as a specified amount of navy tobacco— once a week."

Shimkin says this is partly the way Washakie grew to be such a large figure in Eastern Shoshone lore. "This dazzling prosperity brought many Indians flocking to Washakie's colors," Shimkin wrote. "It was scarcely surprising that 'Shoshones who left the tribe long ago, and other Shoshones, mixed bloods (from Fort Bridger), numbering 46 lodges and 216 souls, have lately been coming into the agency, and ask that they may be permitted to stay and learn to farm.' [according to a Report of the Commissioner of Indian Affairs]."

The help from the government came at a price. The tribe was expected to farm. This plan started out relatively successfully in 1872. "Under white tutelage, the Shoshone had struggled mightily to plow 320 acres with half-wild ponies," wrote Shimkin. "They had then left for their annual summer hunt, returning to find their white friends in charge of a splendid crop that fall." But by 1874 the Shoshone were struggling to grow potatoes in the Wyoming dirt, and by 1876 much of the prairie had reclaimed the farmed land. The fur industry was in the tank, the bison were scarce, and the Arapaho had joined the Shoshone on the rez. Washakie was not without his detractors, some of whom claimed the chief enriched himself by taxing his people. Nevertheless, Washakie and his cadre earned the respect of the whites. "The leaders in these changes were highly intelligent, discriminating, sociable and emotionally acute men with great initiative. Their number is not large in any population," wrote Shimkin.

The number of Eastern Shoshone on the reservation diminished as the problems—grasshoppers, drought, disease, alcoholism, etc—hit the tribe hard, with population numbers only rebounding a bit around 1900. In the meantime, a new hardship was placed on the Native Americans: the separation of children from their parents through the use of boarding schools. The boarding schools—some as far away as Carlisle, PA and Florida—were meant to help Native Americans assimilate into white culture. It also meant banning the language and customs of the tribes. For a people who put a high value on family, this forced separation was very painful. One of the American Indian Relief Council's websites says that the assimilation methods may have been well intentioned. Still, their goal was to teach "the importance of private property, material wealth, and monogamous nuclear families."

The forced education of Native American children in faraway boarding schools created upheaval on the Wind River Reservation. White schools on the reservation were scarcely better, with Native American parents and children separated but in clear view of each other. Mothers could see their children being led from dormitories to the schoolhouse, in line, in order, under strict discipline. Sometimes, parents were forced to make odious decisions. "Indian agents on the reservations normally resorted to withholding rations or sending in agency police to enforce the school policy," the AIRC website reads. "In some cases, police were sent onto the reservations to seize children from their parents, whether willing or not. The police would continue to take children until the school was filled, so sometimes orphans were offered up or families would negotiate a family quota. Navajo police officers avoided taking 'prime' children and would take children assumed to be less intelligent, those not well cared for or those physically impaired."

The kids, sometimes encouraged by the parents, snuck away from the schools, at night or in the summer, and foraged for traditional Native American foods, herbs, and medicines. They would not let go of their ways. Even the boarding schools that were considered more enlightened came down hard on children who tried to hold on to traditions. The headmaster of the Carlisle Indian School in Pennsylvania, Col. Richard Henry Pratt, had a motto: "Kill the Indian, Save the Man."

Native American art continued. At the boarding schools, in jails, and elsewhere, on reservations, artists sought materials with which to create, despite the giant machine pushing assimilation. Traditionally, the men painted and drew on bison hides to tell stories. Narratives about hunts and battles dominated the designs by the men, while the women favored geometric designs. When the bison were driven nearly to extinction, the Native American artists needed a new substrate. The surface that whites were willing to give to them, the painting support that was freely supplied to prisons, schools, and reservation agencies, was ledgers for accounts. Using crayons, ink, and watercolors, the Native Americans drew images that would prove useful to ethnologists and appealing to art

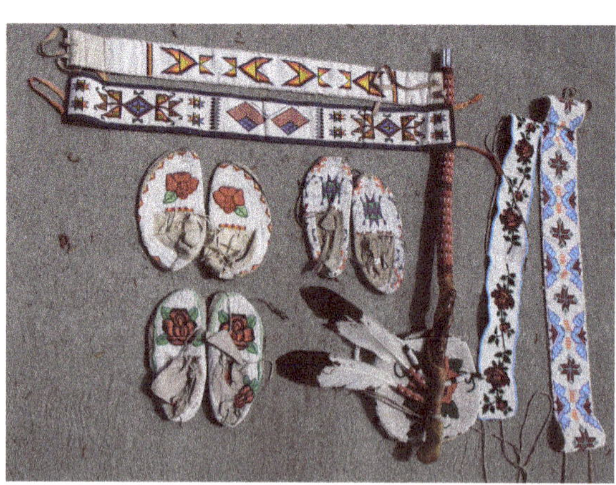

Moccasins, sacred belts and a staff owned by Willie LeClair, an elder on the Wind River Reservation.

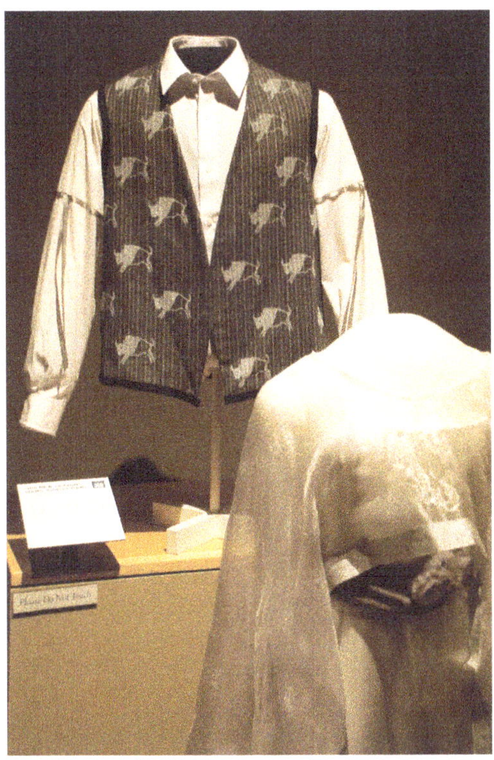

Shirt, vest, and blouse by Gina Still Smoking, a contemporary Lakota artist. Below: Detail of blouse design.

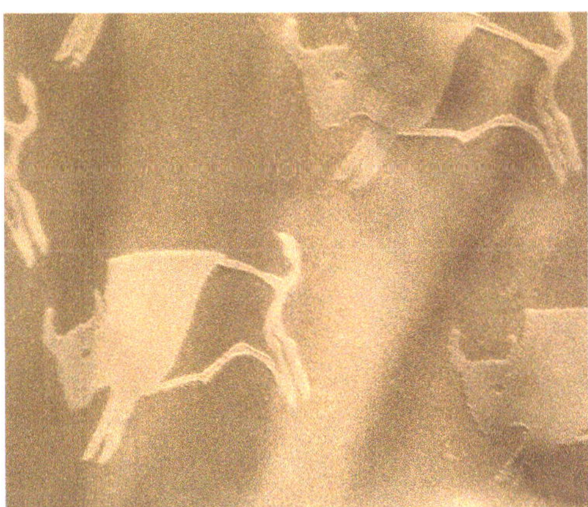

collectors.

Today some Native American artists mark that period in history by continuing to create art on old ledger paper, old deeds, and similar substrates. The materials used remind viewers of the time when ledgers were their only option. The new artwork allows the Native American artist to transform the ledger tradition, to address contemporary audiences with both new ideas and events from the past that should not be forgotten.

On the Wind River Reservation, the alarm has long sounded to alert people to preserve and understand the tribes' traditions, but the consumer culture is engineered to titillate and captivate. Few young persons of any kind can resist the siren song of electronics and media. "As educators, our job is to guide people who are fluent in both worlds, says Cleve Bell, the art teacher at Wyoming Indian High School, in Ethete. "There is a way for those two to coexist and to be in harmony. Here, we are the melting pot of the melting pot. It's really hard to compete with modern technology, with the music and the devices—it's very seductive. Kids are searching for identity and they take on what there's the most of. A lot of kids are still raised in the Native American culture of their family and stick to it. But if you aren't raised in it, it's really hard to hang on to it."

Echoes a Shoshone elder, "There is so much unknown that should be known of legend and tradition. We are losing it, because we don't have the older people anymore. They are passing away. A lot of it comes into finding the people who are going to be telling you accurate information. You don't know when you are going to get it. Then it's put on your plate and the next thing, you are that."

Some Native American artists keep tradition alive by crafting pots, moccasins, ceremonial tools, headdresses, and other traditional items. Non-natives tend to value older artifacts over newly minted creations, but the legacy lives. "The earliest artifacts in this area are pottery," says an elder. "It was utilitarian, but it was more than functional. They made the pots beautiful."

In terms of dazzling beauty, nothing beats the objects created for the popular powwows attended by many Native Americans. The clothes, the staffs, the fans, the headdresses, the moccasins, weapons—all are possible vehicles for carefully chosen and attached feathers, beads, and sinew.

Ben Pease standing beside one of his paintings on display at the Plains Museum in the Buffalo Bill Center of the West, in Cody, Wyoming.

"I was raised in Oklahoma and went to powwows most weekends," says Bell. "It was amazing, and it is why I am an artist right now. Some people spend all their money and time making costumes, doing the beadwork. It's not uncommon to see people at a powwow creating a new costume for the next powwow. For some, it's a nomadic lifestyle, following the powwows. You can make good money. It's such a great time, too."

Another group of Native American artists take this history of adorning clothes, tools, and weapons and twists it in a more obviously contemporary way. Consider the textile work of Gina StillSmoking, who makes men's suits and women's dresses with patterns that are unmistakably Native. Or the surprising hip-hop elements incorporated into Robert Martinez's paintings. Or the dreamlike blend of old and new in Ben Pease's arresting work.

"I use old imagery that readdresses tradition," Louis Still Smoking states about his bracingly modern paintings. Geometric shapes, primary colors that fit well in Native American tradition, contemporary scenes that link to the past—Louis' art is a good example of new traditions in art among Native Americans.

Pease would be upset if a viewer felt excluded from the images put forth by this group of artists, who call themselves the Creative Indigenous Collective. "My artwork is for everyone," he says. The collective recently enjoyed two significant museum shows—one at the Hockaday Museum of Art, in Kalispell, Montana, and the other at the Plains Indian Museum at the Buffalo Bill Center of the West, in Cody, Wyoming. With wide exposure from continuing museum shows, the collective's work seems destined for a wide audience—made up of people from many cultures. Native American art endures in the Rockies. It has never been divorced from the greater tribal culture.

Chapter 4

Early Explorers, Trappers, and Alfred Jacob Miller:
Undiscovered Country
(1742-1849)

The Wind River Valley and the Greater Yellowstone area has long been a fruitful hunting ground for humans, but in the mid-1700s, back in Washington, DC's halls of power and in the offices of intrepid business owners, it was still considered an undiscovered country, pregnant with possibility and hardscrabble adventure. White Americans of European descent had pushed in toward the area from the east, west, and north, but few had penetrated the Rocky Mountains as far as the Wind River and Teton ranges. Some sources mark the French Canadian brothers Louis-Joseph de la Gaultier de La Vérendrye and François de La Vérendrye as the first

whites to explore the upper Wind River Valley in 1742 or 1743; this is almost assuredly not so. More than likely, the first to see the Pinnacles, Gannett Peak, or the Ramshorn was a freelance trapper— or perhaps a Russian trapper from Alaska. The Vérendryes evidently did travel south from Manitoba, and according to the journal of the father of the Vérendrye brothers, enter the land of the Snake people (the Shoshone). Some sources interpret the journal accounts as saying the brothers came up the Wind River and crossed over the Winds to winter in the Green River Valley

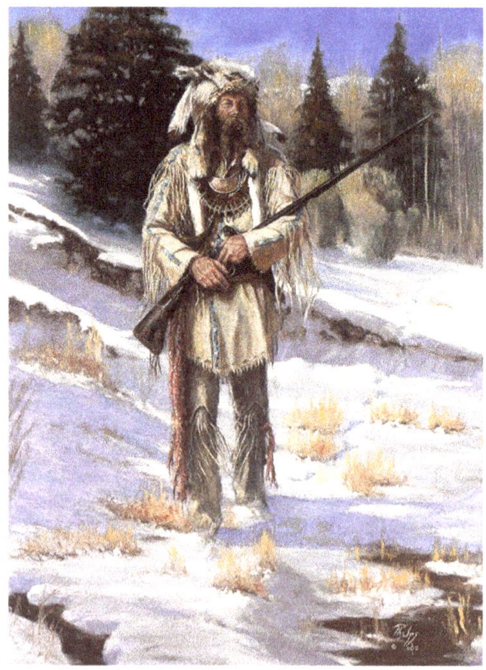

"Mountain Man," by John Phelps,
oil, 40 x 30 in.

in 1743. The landmarks described in the journal, and the tribes mentioned, suggest a certain route for the Vérendrye brothers, but their astrolabe had broken, so there's no dependable location data.

Indeed, in general the records are scant and the evidence is open to interpretation. Thus, we are left with two groups of people: those who only deal with the incontrovertibly proven, and those who are willing to deal in probabilities. The latter assert that the first whites to see this land were probably unknown trappers, working their territory in anonymity. Those who are unwilling to speculate beyond written records and other sources will only say the Vérendrye brothers were the first recorded whites in the Greater Yellowstone area. Choose your tribe and think accordingly.

The Vérendryes were fur traders, and it was the pelts of beavers that drove their first explorations of the Wind River mountains and valley. The Wind River Valley was, at the time, territory in dispute between the Crow and the Shoshone. In the middle of this—sometimes benefitting from the dispute and sometimes falling afoul of it—were trappers. Trappers, especially the itinerant kind who were at home in the wilderness, were sometimes called mountain men in that part of the Rockies.

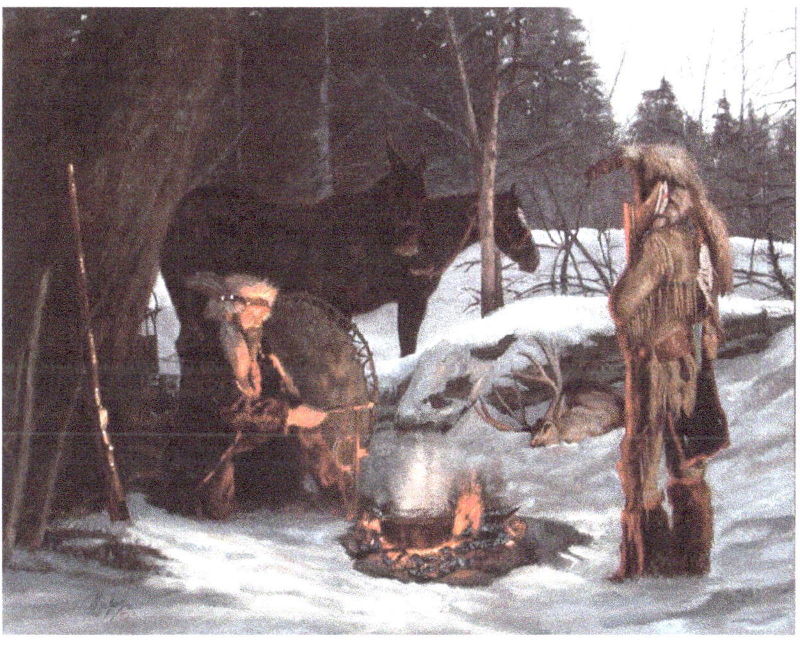

"Boiling the Traps," by John Phelps, oil.

The mountain man is a familiar character in American culture, although the type is often misrepresented. "There were no old mountain men," artist and Western culture expert John Phelps asserts, by which he means that staying alive in the Rockies on one's own is a job for young people. It was a rough life that asked much from a human. Mountain men usually died or "retired" to some other occupation as they grew older. The true mountain men often worked alone, coming together with others only for strategic reasons of trapping or to sell the pelts they gathered. Historian Nolie Mumey writes, "According to [trapper and U.S. Army officer Benjamin Louis Eulalie de] Bonneville, the free trappers of the West lived the most dangerous, strenuous, and exciting life of any class of people. They defied the Indians, torrents, inclement weather, and wild beasts. They could be seen, at times, searching routes inaccessible to the horse, crossing streams, and scaling rugged mountains, ever looking for new places where they might meet their favorite game. This was a typical picture of the trappers."

Beaver fur had been a popular material for hats in Europe since 1550, and trapping was enthusiastically pursued from the Hudson Bay, down through New York, and across the continent (U.S. Midwest) through Illinois, and again over in the Pacific Northwest. The Rockies were relatively untapped and unmapped. The French Canadians and the English were eager to claim more territory for trapping, and they both eyed the mountains of Wyoming, then a part of Oregon Territory. This foreign interest got the attention of U.S. President Thomas Jefferson.

Jefferson was intent on expanding the United States. In 1803 Jefferson extended the country's boundaries by 828,000 square miles through the Louisiana Purchase, a deal with the French costing about $245 million in 2017 dollars and gaining a swath of land stretching from New Orleans to Saskatchewan. Large chunks of Wyoming and Montana were part of that purchase. Meanwhile, disturbing news about the British lit another fire under Jefferson's seat. Historian Carl Parcher Russell writes that Jefferson and Congress were riled up about Northwest explorer Alexander Mackenzie's public call for Britain to expand its territory from the Atlantic to the Pacific so "the entire command of the fur trade of North America might be obtained from 48 degrees north to the pole. ... Such would be the field for commercial enterprise and incalculable would be the produce of it." Jefferson immediately set about planning an expedition to find a Northwest Passage across the continent, right through the Rockies of present-day Wyoming, with both commerce and scientific inquiry on his mind.

The resulting expedition was headed by Meriwether Lewis, an Army captain who showed an ability and affinity for learning. In preparation for his quest, Jefferson tutored Lewis on many subjects at his home at Monticello, and sent him to study with Philadelphia physician Benjamin Rush to learn basic medicine. Additionally, he received instruction in astronomy—enabling Lewis to correctly navigate by the stars—from Andrew Ellicott.

The next step was forming his party, a group who became known as the Corps of Discovery. Lewis had once served under Lieutenant William Clark, a frontiersman based in Kentucky, and spurred by Lewis's need for dependable leaders for the Corps, the two met outside of Louisville, where Lewis asked Clark to co-command the expedition. More than a third of the rest of the party were Kentuckians who had experience in the woods, experience with both peaceful and hostile relations with Native Americans, and knew trapping, according to Russell. The expedition gathered in St. Louis and embarked on their journey on May 14, 1804 at 4 p.m. from a military outpost named, coincidentally, Camp Dubois [Camp Wood].

The Lewis and Clark expedition was a success, one that created a stir back East. The Corps made significant strides in establishing relations with Native American tribes, in mapping the country, and in the study of plants, animals, and minerals from the

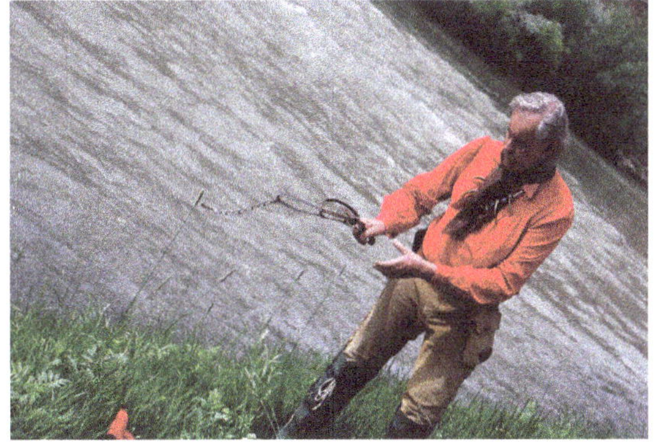

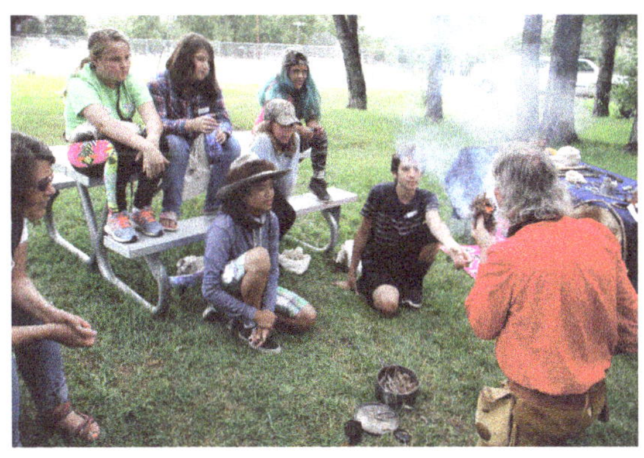

Steve Banks, a Dubois historian, demonstrates how mountain men set a beaver trap (top) and how to start a fire using traditional methods.

region. The trip constitutes an adventure story better than most fictional tales; a good book for reading about the Corps of Discovery is Stephen E. Ambrose's 1996 work *Undaunted Courage: Meriwether Lewis, Thomas Jefferson, and the Opening of the American West.* To survive the trip, the company needed to have some of the savvy of the trappers. "The Lewis and Clark party, so long and so far removed from civilized sources of supply, 'lived off the land,'" writes Russell. "Understandably, the meat of wild animals constituted a major item in the larder, and the skill of the hunter and the worthiness of his gun were more than chatty after-supper topics."

And skills they had. In The Journals of Lewis and Clark, the entry for Feb. 13, 1805 describes how they split up to hunt while staying at their winter camp in North Dakota. Clark came back with 36 deer and 14 elk. Lewis came back with more than 3,000 pounds of meat—dressed and deboned in the field. Russell writes, "Game was plentiful…and was more a trial of physical strength and endurance than a test of guns and the hunter's skills. Later, during the expedition's long march, there were numerous occasions when game was scarce and it was then that the hunting prowess of certain backwoodsmen in the party came to the fore."

One member of the Corps of Discovery was Private John Colter, a Kentuckian and skilled hunter and woodsman. Colter went on to become one of the most famous trappers and guides of the Rockies, but his start out

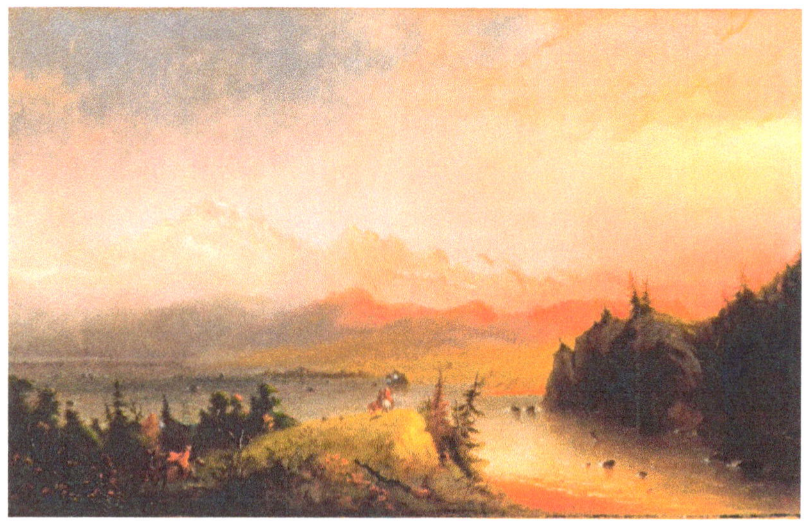

"Trappers Saluting the Wind River Mountains,"
by Alfred Jacob Miller, oil, 25 x 39 in.

West was on the Lewis and Clark expedition. Lewis and Clark are known to every schoolchild in the United States (we hope), but there are some who say stopping the story there forgets about the trappers who kept the West open. "This is how the West was expanded," asserts Stephen Banks. "Lewis and Clark did not accomplish what Jefferson wanted. He was going to get his nation to stretch from one coast to another. And this was the gap, right here."

John Colter may not have been thinking so grandiose. He smelled a fortune to be made.

On the return trip from the mouth of the Columbia River at the Pacific Ocean, Colter asked if he could leave the Corps of Discovery. In *The Journals of Lewis and Clark,* the entry for Aug. 15-16, 1806 reads, "In the evening we were appealed to by one of our men, Colter, who was desirous of joining the two trappers who had accompanied us and who now proposed an expedition up the river, in which they were to find traps and give Colter a share of the profits. The offer was a very advantageous one, and, as he had always performed his duty, and his services might be dispensed with, we agreed that he might go, providing none of the others would ask or expect a similar indulgence. To this they cheerfully answered that they wished Colter

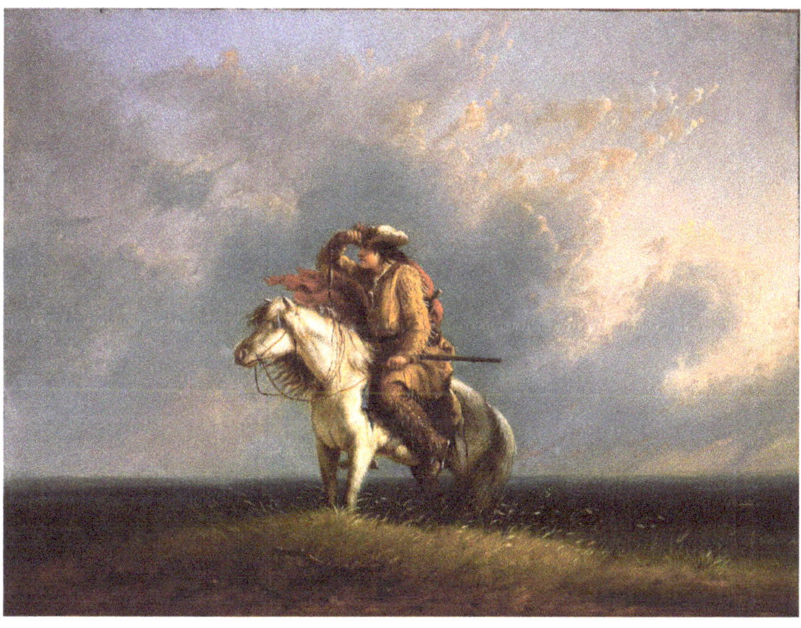

"Lost Greenhorn," by A. J. Miller

every success and would not apply for liberty to separate before we reached St. Louis. We, therefore, supplied him (as did his comrades) with powder, lead, and a variety of articles which might be useful to him, and he left us the next day."

Some in the Corps were flabbergasted that Colter would want to go it alone in that wild country. "The example of this man shows how easily men may be weaned from the habits of a civilized life to the ruder, but scarcely less fascinating manners of the woods," reads an entry in Nicholas Biddle's edit of *The Journals of Lewis and Clark*. "This hunter had now been absent for many years from the frontiers, and might naturally be presumed to have some anxiety, or some curiosity at least to return to his friends and his country; yet just at the moment when he is approaching the frontiers, he is tempted by a hunting scheme, to give up those delightful prospects, and go back without the least reluctance to the solitude of the woods."

According to Burton Harris's 1993 book on Colter, it's not terribly shocking that the other men in the Corps of Discovery were surprised by Colter's decision. Harris asserts that trappers were not held in high esteem by other whites, that they were considered to have "gone native." The trappers dealt with game nearly every day, and as a result, they reportedly smelled bad— and they didn't know it. Perhaps it shouldn't be surprising that hygiene and fashion were compromised in the trapper's life. Form follows function, and the rugged mountains of Wyoming require one to function at a high and spare level to stay alive.

It was Colter who later followed the Wind River all the way to its headwaters, allegedly crossing Togwotee Pass in 1807, breaking open some of the last territory unknown to whites back East. "He explored the sources of the Snake River and climbed a portion of the Teton Mountains," writes Nolie Mumey. "He discovered the regions which have since been named Wind River Range, Union Pass, Jackson's Hole [sic], Teton Pass, Pierre's Hole, and the Three Tetons, as well as the headwaters of the Colorado of the West."

Colter's 500-mile solo hike went through mountains that would challenge experienced hikers today. (It should also be said, however, that people well acquainted with this area's terrain and climate doubt that Colter went through Togwotee Pass in winter 1807 on foot, but rather, came over the Bighorns and routed around Thermopolis.) His journey was on the behalf of St. Louis fur trader Manuel Lisa. The idea was to advertise what kind of trading and supplies could be had at Fort Lisa, which was then located in

North Dakota. Colter carried a 30-pound pack of goods and supplies, with plenty of gifts for Native Americans he'd encounter along the way. Like any hiker, Colter was careful to carry as few heavy items as possible. To that end, he took just enough tobacco and knives (heavy), and an abundance of beads, awls, and needles.

In 1808 Colter took on a partner, John Potts, who was also a member of the Corps of Discovery. Together they sought trade agreements with Native American nations on behalf of Fort Raymond's trapping trade, primarily dealing with the Flatheads and Crows. This was the prologue to one of the greatest stories of the U.S. frontier.

In 1809, Potts and Colter were setting traps on the Jefferson River, which is located in Montana west of Bozeman, northwest of Yellowstone National Park. They knew the area was used by the Blackfoot people, who had a lethal aversion to white men since a member of Lewis and Clark's party killed two Blackfoot braves on July 27, 1806 in central Montana. What followed was an episode, known as Colter's Run, that has been told many times since the actual events transpired. Some versions glorify John Colter, some offer apologies for the behavior of John Potts, some embrace clear historical inaccuracies, and many of the rest happily express the beloved skill early trappers and mountain men had to embellish the truth. Here, culled from several historical sources, is a version that honors all of those

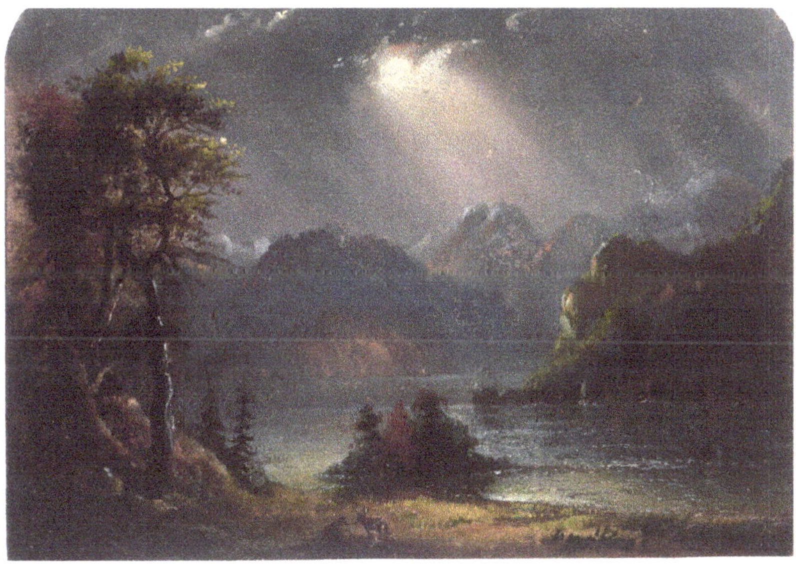

"Storm on Wind River Lake, Rocky Mountains," by Alfred Jacob Miller, oil, 7 x 10 in.

approaches, brought together—perhaps in a wholly unholy way--for the sake of the tale--and what a tale it is.

Colter and Potts were moving along the Jefferson River as stealthily as possible, setting or checking traps. But not stealthily enough. They were caught by as many as 800 Blackfoot, who lined the shore and demanded that the two land their canoe. Colter believed the Blackfoot were simply going to relieve them of their possessions. Potts was having none of it. Accounts vary at this point. We'll be generous and embrace the most flattering to Potts.

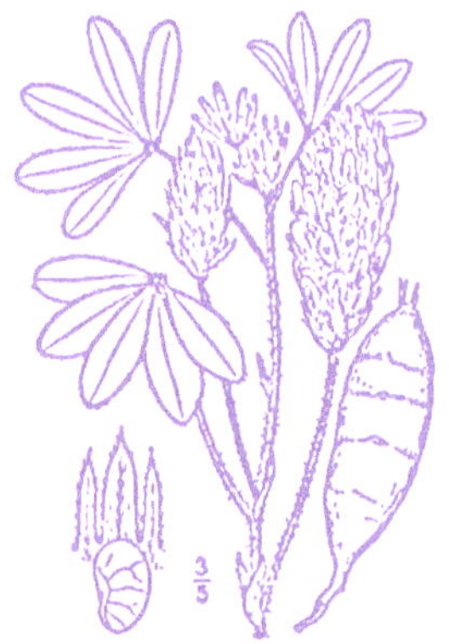

Colter waded ashore, and the Blackfoot stripped him. Potts refused to follow, and an arrow found its way into his leg. "Are you hurt?" Colter asked. "Yes, too much hurt to escape; if you can get away, do so," replied Potts. "I will kill at least one of them." And indeed, he took a Pott-shot at a brave, killing him, and was immediately "riddled with arrows." According to one account, the Blackfoot then dragged him ashore, hacked Potts to pieces with hatchets and knives, and threw his entrails, heart, lungs, etc in Colter's face. The relatives of the murdered Blackfoot were "furious with rage and struggled, tomahawk in hand, to reach Colter, while others held them back." Colter was brought in front of a chief, who asked him if he were a fast runner. Colter lied and said no. The chief indicated that he was to run.

According to one account, the chief merely said "Go—go away." Colter started walking, but when he saw the braves removing their blankets, leggings, etc, he knew it was a race. "He ran with all the speed that nature,

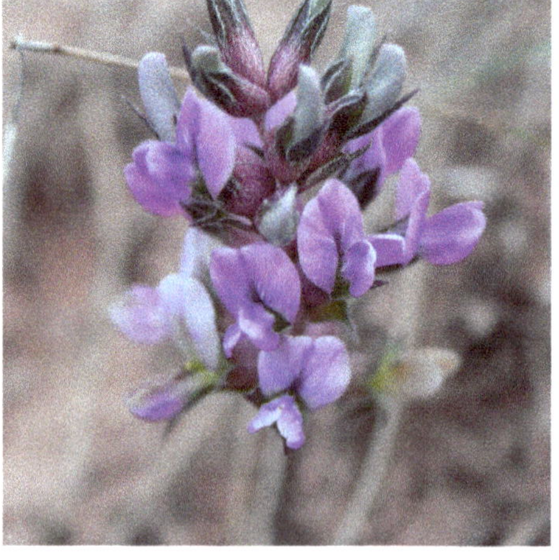

Psoralea esculenta, *commonly known as breadroot or prairie turnip.*

excited to the utmost, could give; fear and hope lent a supernatural vigor to his limbs and the rapidity of his flight astonished himself," the account says. He ran five miles through rough country, stepping on prickly pear cactus and rocks, pushing himself so hard that his nose began to bleed from the exertion. Most of the braves were left behind, but one was gaining on him. When the brave was within 60 feet, Colter, in desperation, stopped and turned toward the Blackfoot, raising his arms. The move surprised the brave (and perhaps Colter's bloody countenance did, too), and he quickly started to throw his spear at Colter. But he stumbled forward while doing so, catching the spear in the ground and falling, in the process breaking the shaft of the spear. Colter quickly picked up the short end with the point and "pinned him to the ground." And he ran on.

Colter came to the Madison River and jumped in, looking for cover. He spied a beaver lodge [a notion challenged by some, who suspect it was a raft of sorts made of driftwood] and swam under it to take refuge. The rest of the braves soon arrived, howling in fury, and searched for him, at times standing on the deadfall, visible above Colter through the sticks.

When night came, the Blackfoot gave up the search, and Colter swam down the river a ways. "Fearing that the Indians might have guarded the pass, which was the only outlet from the valley, and to avoid the danger of surprise, Colter ascended the almost perpendicular mountain before him, the tops and sides covered by perpetual snow. He had no weapon, food, or clothes—just a blanket he had taken from the fallen Blackfoot. By morning he had reached the top. It was 300 miles to the nearest fort. He had to endure the sun, but after traveling 11 days he made it to Ft. Manuel. He survived on psoralea esculenta, commonly known as breadroot or the prairie turnip. Wikipedia defines it thusly: "As a food, the prairie turnip has been described variously as a 'delicacy,' 'tolerably good eating,' or 'tasteless and insipid.'" The Indian's use of it as food is described as follows: "They eat it uncooked, or they boil it, or roast it in the embers, or dry it, and crush it to powder and make soup of it. Large quantities are stored in buffalo skin bags for winter use. A sort of pudding made of the flour of the roots and the maseskatomina (saskatoon) berry is very palatable and a favorite dish."

In 1810 Colter turned his back on the Western wilderness and returned to St. Louis, where he married and bought a farm. He fought in the War of 1812 and died of jaundice in 1813.

Meanwhile, the beaver trade continued to thrive. John Jacob Astor, who was America's first multi-millionaire, built a fur trading business with assets in

Canada, the Great Lakes Region, and the Pacific Northwest. Astor funded an expedition led by William Price Hunt that went through Union Pass on Sept. 16, 1811. The journey was part of Astor's research to determine where to build trading posts and generally scope out the land.

The War of 1812 disrupted the fur trade, as Britain supplied guns and other supplies to Native American tribes and urged them to attack American settlements and frontiersmen. The war also ended the cooperation (or tolerance) that had previously presided over trapping by various nations in "British America"—Canada. The war was fully over in January of 1815 when American forces won the Battle of New Orleans and salved the nation's pride, which had been bruised by defeats at the Siege of Detroit and the Battle of Queenston Heights. Trappers and explorers turned back to business.

Astor funded another landmark expedition in 1832, led by Benjamin Louis Eulalie de Bonneville. Bonneville and 110 men set out from Missouri to build business for Astor, but he encountered reluctance among the Native Americans he met, who were afraid of endangering their business with the Hudson Bay Company, Astor's rival. By summer of 1833 he was exploring the Wind River Mountains and trading with the local Shoshone with some success. His venture further cracked open the Winds to organized commerce, and furthered the industry of trapping in the area.

The Wind River Mountains were still wild, promising unpredictable encounters with the Native Americans and the very real threat of death from weather and wild animals. In 1834 Kit Carson was hunting elk alone and was chased up a tree by two grizzlies. One stayed around a long time, shaking the tree to try to knock Carson down. Carson wrote that the bear "finally concluded to leave, of which I was heartily pleased, never having been so scared in my life."

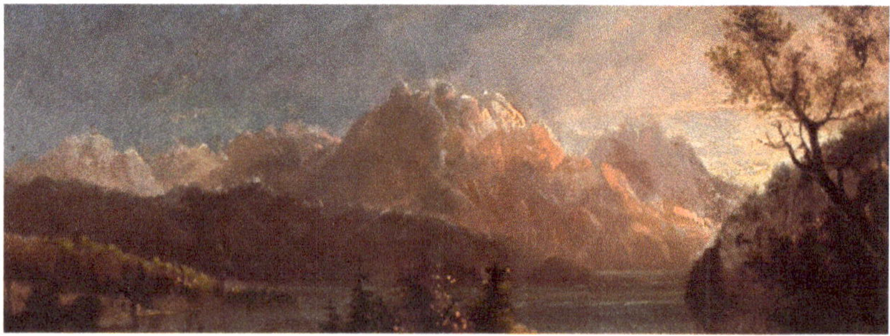

"Wind River Mountains, Night," by Alfred Jacob Miller, oil, 7 x 10 in.

Visual art in the Wind River Mountains was limited to the craftsmanship of the area's Native Americans. At this point, nearly all of the few white travelers in the region were hunters and trappers. And, as Mumey put it, "It is doubtful that the early trappers looked at nature with an artist's eye and appreciated the rugged beauty of the mountains. In their practical, hard-working life they may often have tired of the rugged range which caused the many weary climbs."

But at least one explorer had noticed the charm of the Winds. Sir William Drummond Stewart, the heir to a baronetcy in Scotland, traveled through Western Wyoming in the 1830s, and he cut quite an interesting figure in doing so. His story is entwined with the first white artist to capture artful impressions of the Wind River Mountains, and it is a story worth telling.

It's 1837 in Baltimore, Maryland, and a young artist is hungry, ambitious, and feeling the need to get out of town. He had recently returned from study in Europe, where he was accepted in Paris's École des Beaux Arts, and he had copied pieces by Rembrandt, Delacroix, Titan, Raphael, Turner, and Correggio that he saw in France, Italy, and Switzerland. Back home in Baltimore, he was learning the portrait business. However, he decided to move to New Orleans, for reasons now unclear. Perhaps he still had the itch to travel, maybe he wished to be free from romantic or familial entanglements, or he was not satisfied with the prospects of his portrait business.

The artist described his situation thusly, "A young man left his home to seek a fortune in New Orleans. Trouble of all kinds had accumulated and in order not to be burdensome, engaged passage on a merchant ship and in a week reached his destination with $30 in his pocket."

His name was Alfred Jacob Miller. He rented a studio in the French Quarter and painted a portrait of his landlord, who was sufficiently impressed to recommend Miller to acquaintances who may want their likeness painted. But not long after he set up shop, a visitor stopped by his studio to examine his work, and Miller's life changed.

In a journal, Miller wrote, "One day while busily engaged on a picture in my room on Chartres St. New Orleans, a gentleman walked in and after nodding to me commenced examining the pictures on the walls, consisting of portraits and landscapes, framed and otherwise. At first glance he seemed to be a Kentuckian—he held himself as straight as an arrow (to be sure, there was no Bowie knife peeping out at the top of his vest—this formed very fashionable jewelry at that time on the lower border of the Mississippi) and he had a military air."

"The gentleman mentioned previous, in a few days after, called again," he continued. "This time he was more sociable—took a chair and after a little conversation handed me a card on which was engraved 'Capt. W. D. Stewart, British Army.' He then told me that he was making preparations for another journey to the Rocky Mountains (he had already made two or three) and wished to have a competent artist to sketch the remarkable scenery and incidents of the journey. 'Now,' he said, 'as I am very well satisfied with your work I should like you to accompany me. Take a little time to think over it, and also call on the British Consul here, Mr. Crawford. He will give you any information that you may require as regards myself. Also consult your friends.' I called on Mr. Crawford and he gave me to understand that Capt. Stewart was the next heir to the vast estate of Murthly in Scotland, that he made these journeys for his pleasure and instruction, and advised me by all means to accept his kind offer, which I eventually did."

Stewart was an interesting character. He enthusiastically joined the British Army and served under Wellington. His brother inherited his father's estate, but he was sickly, and Stewart knew that he needed to be ready to assume his father's title. Being of an adventurous sort, he toured the rugged West of the United States before his obligations called for him to manage things in Scotland. After attending a trapper's rendezvous in 1833, Stewart was hooked on both the wild country and the intrepid people who lived and hunted in the Rockies.

One can hardly blame Stewart for admiring the pageantry and drama of a trapper's rendezvous. Here's how Ron Tyler described Stewart's experience, in his Gerald Peters Gallery essay for a Miller expedition: "The 1833 rendezvous, four miles north of Horse Creek on the Green River in what is today southwestern Wyoming, was like nothing else that Stewart had ever seen: hundreds of Indian teepees clustered unevenly throughout the valley; Indians, free trappers, company men, and traders frolicking amidst horse races, powwows, and occasional 'rough and tumble' fights. The traders quickly obtained the beaver pelts and buffalo robes from the trappers and Indians, then spent the rest of the time selling their goods to the newly flush customers."

Four years later, the rendezvous seemed to have grown, and Miller was there to document it. "At certain specified times during the year, the American Fur Company appoints a 'Rendezvous' at particular localities (selecting the most available spots) for the purpose of trading with Indians and Trappers, and here they congregate from all corners. While at Rendezvous we were summoned at intervals to see the Indians perform their dances, engage in ball play, and test their bows and skills in shooting at a mark," Miller later wrote. "In order to give free action, they throw off their robe, retaining a cloth around their hips which they ornament in various ways with feathers, etc. Sometimes a bull's tail is secured to the rest as if they thought nature had omitted this appendage; and it is possible Lord Monboddo founded his wild theory that people existed who had tails from some such savage trick as this…. To the left, seated is an arrow maker, busily engaged in preparing and pointing shafts, made usually from the Cotton-wood tree, on account of its lightness, and being easily worked. Great care is taken in having the arrow well balanced, straight, and uniform throughout, as on this depends the directness of its flight and aim."

The Rocky Mountain Rendezvous gathered trappers and traders together in the Wyoming area every spring-summer from 1825 to 1840. The location changed, wandering as far as Pierre's Hole, Idaho; Bear Lake and Cache Valley, Utah; and in various points in Wyoming, from Lander to Riverton to Granger and McKinnon. Rendezvous were held six times in Daniel, Wyoming, near the Green River. The 1837 Rendezvous was one of the last big Rendezvous, and Miller was there in the Green River Valley with Stewart to witness it. His 69"-x-96" canvas "Cavalcade" depicts the ceremonial parade that opened the event.

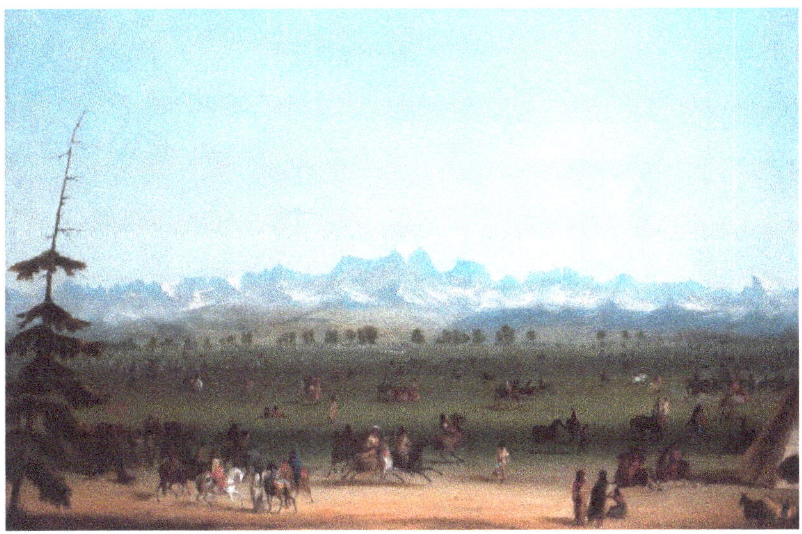

"Rendezvous," by Alfred Jacob Miller, oil, 32 x 38 in.

"Here we encamped for a month in the midst of upwards of two thousand Snake Indians [Shoshone], who were friendly and hospitable," Miller reported. "The cavalcade was projected in honor of our Leader's arrival amongst them, and was extremely unique and interesting. The Indian chief, Ma-wo-ma, rode in front, while the main body followed without any military order or platooning. Some of the dresses worn were magnificent, and although vermillion was worth four dollars per ounce, a lavish use of that article was exhibited on their bodies and faces. The Snakes in comparison with other tribes may be considered in affluent circumstances—they have a large supply of fine horses and live in a district abounding with game, have the finest lodges we saw, and impressed us more than any other tribe with their courteous and friendly manners."

In describing another scene he painted, Miller says, "A large body of Indians, Traders, and Trappers are here congregated, and the view seen from a bluff is pleasing and animated. In the middle distance, a race is being run, the horses in all cases running in a direct line and never in a circle as with us. The bets pending on the result are extraordinary in character and diversity, and the Indians are passionately fond of this species of gambling. If an Indian happens to lose all, he will stake the dress he wears against 3 or 4 ounces of vermillion and if you win can demand it at once, leaving him almost in the condition of Adam before the Fall. The Company's tent is besieged on such occasions. No matter who loses, they are sure to win.

"Ball playing with bandys [field hockey sticks] and other games are largely indulged in, and the Company makes it a point to encourage the Indians in these sports to divert their minds from mischief," Miller continues. "White lodges ranging from 12 to 16 feet in height are scattered at random over the

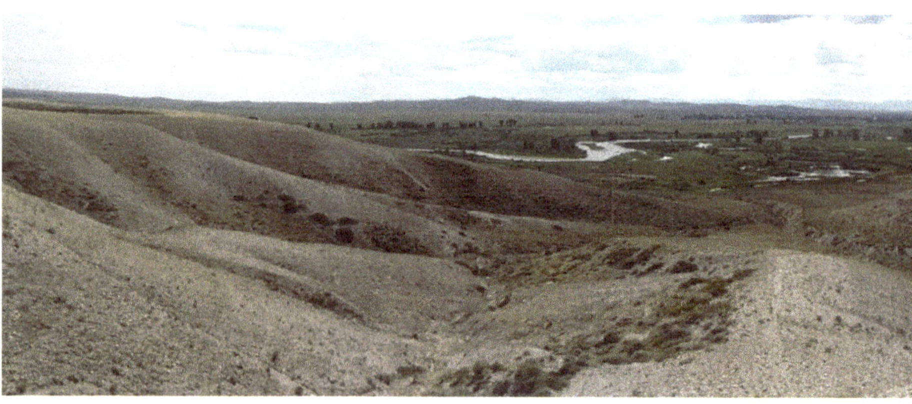

Panorama view of the rendezvous site in the Green River Valley near Daniel, Wyoming.

plain and reach almost to the foot of the distant mountains.

"The first day is devoted to 'High Jinks,' a species of Saturnalia, in which feasting, drinking, and gambling form prominent parts…. Sometimes an Indian becomes so excited with 'Fire Water' that he commences 'running a muck'—he is pursued, thrown, or knocked down, and secured, in order to keep him from mischief. 'Affairs of honor' now and then are adjusted between rival Trappers—one of the parties, of course, receiving a complete drubbing, all caused evidently from mixing too much alcohol with their water. Night closes this scene with revelry and confusion. The following days exhibit the strongest contrast to this. The Fur Company's great tent is raised, the Indians erect their picturesque white lodges, the accumulated furs of the hunting season are brought forth, and the Company's tent is a besieged and busy place. Now the women come in for their share of ornaments and finery, being as Tony Lumpkin expresses it, 'in a con-cat-enation accordingly.' The free trapper most especially bestowing presents on his favorite regardless of expense."

The Native Americans inspired much curiosity in Miller, but they had to compete with some other big personalities in attendance, including Jim Bridger. For a while, Bridger was not only a famous trapper, he was a trapper executive, one of the owners of Rocky Mountain Fur Company. His demeanor at the 1837 Rendezvous was appropriately splendid. Miller reports seeing the plain in front of him dotted with lodges and tents. "In the midst of them is Capt. Bridger in a full suit of steel armor. This gentleman was a famous mountain man, and we venture to say that no one has travelled here within the last 30 years without seeing or hearing of him. The suit of armor was imported from England and presented to Capt. B by our

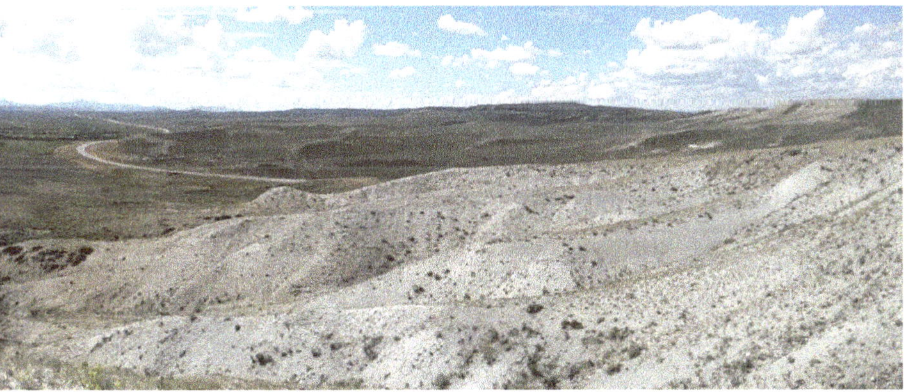

commander; it was a facsimile of that worn by the English life-guards, and created a sensation when worn by him on stated occasions."

The heyday for beaver trappers was brief; by 1842 the fur trade had become much less lucrative. But while the craze for beaver fur was at its height, the Rendezvous was the event of the year in the West. With each year, the footprint of the white man was growing and leaving a lasting mark on the Winds and the West. Kit Carson and Jim Bridger came from St. Louis to Green River on a prospecting trip in fall 1849, further opening Wyoming up for speculation. Around this time, reports of Yellowstone's wonders caused a big stir in St. Louis, and interest in this relatively unknown part of the West increased dramatically. With interest came abuse; a Bridger expedition in 1855 reportedly killed 6,000 buffalo, only taking the tongues "and a little choice meat." Congress was outraged and passed a law prohibiting such slaughter… but there was no one to enforce it in the West, writes E. S. Topping in his *Natural History of Western Wild Animals and Guide for Hunters, Trappers, and Sportsmen*. The West, as it had been in Northwestern Wyoming, was changing, but the government's reach was still further than its grasp.

But in 1837, Miller had ample time to experience the Winds as the Native Americans and the early trappers knew them, wild, difficult, and beautiful. He was arguably the first trained artist to visit the Winds, and he performed predictably, as both greenhorn and expert. Miller's famous piece "The Lost Greenhorn" is sometimes viewed as a psychological self-portrait. Still, it is a bit misleading to view Miller as a pampered artist better suited for the city life he knew in Baltimore. America had an enormous frontier at the time, and Americans of the era were better equipped to venture into the wild than they are now. How many Brooklyn artists today know how to start a fire in the wilderness, fire a gun, or fashion a fishing line and hook well enough to survive on the creatures of the nearest creek? Miller was game as an explorer, and he was also cognizant of the opportunity before him and its significance.

Read any of Miller's descriptions of the landscape, and one can keenly feel his love for the land. "Silence reigned supreme over this beautiful sheet of water, only at long intervals broken by the descent of an avalanche, crashing through the trees and among the rocks," Miller wrote about a mountain lake. "As we viewed these lakes a single line of Keats' occurred to us wherein he says, 'A thing of beauty is a joy forever.' And truly it is so! –It would require but a slight stretch of imagination to fancy the myriads of people in the next generation flocking to see these sublime scenes."

George Catlin and Karl Bodmer depicted Native Americans of the West before Miller did, but according to Ron Tyler, "Miller, by comparison, relied on his Romantic training and inclinations to produce a record of an idyllic summer in the mountains of the Winds that his patron as well as later clients and public would treasure. And because he was the only artist to see the Rendezvous, his paintings have forever fixed that image in our minds."

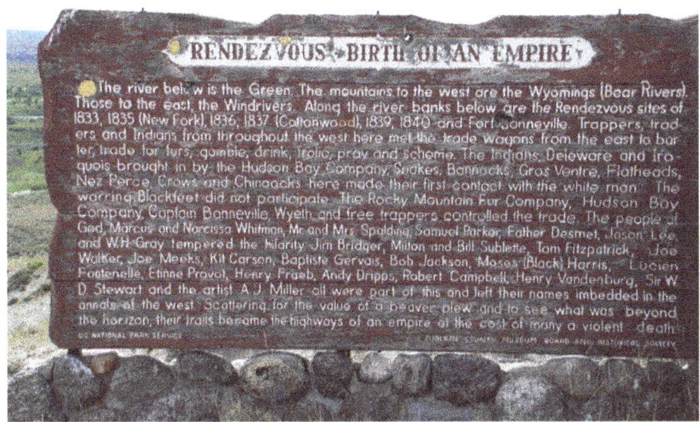

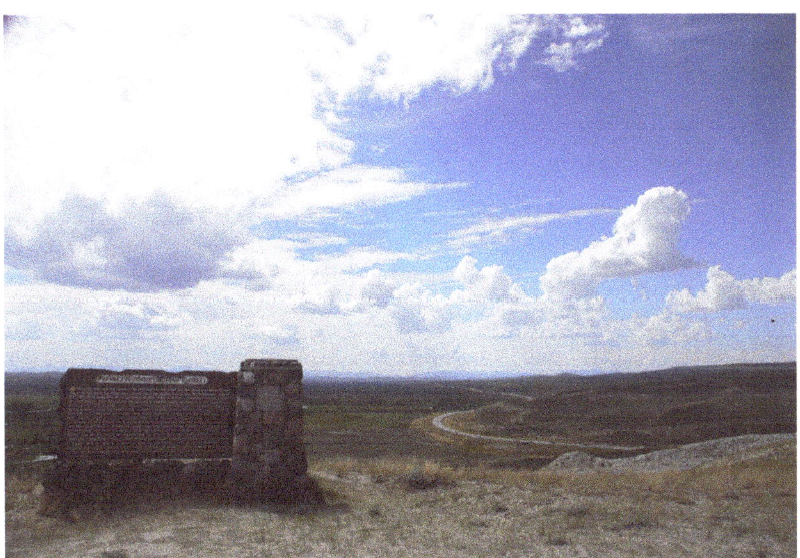

Rendezvous site and National Park Service marker.

Miller was changed by the Winds. He called them "remote and enchanting," a phrase that aptly described the reaction of most artists to explore the area—and for many modern visitors discovering the Wind River Mountains for themselves today. "It was in the Wind River Mountains that Miller saw the most spectacular landscapes of the whole journey," Marvin C. Ross wrote in *The West of Alfred Jacob Miller*. "He realized that he lacked the ability to capture them, either in paint or in words, but his eyes took in the 'deep purple masses,' 'the salmon-colored granite rock,' and the 'immense sheets of clear water' as he dabbed his watercolor brush on the sketching paper. Europe, Greece, Egypt—their wonders have been 'done to death,' he said, but 'here is a new field for…the enterprising traveller…. These mountain Lakes have been waiting for him for thousands of years, and could afford to wait thousands of years longer, for they are now as fresh and beautiful as if just from the hands of the Creator.'"

This trip was the only major one that Miller took out West. In his forlorn goodbyes to some of the sights, one feels that Miller sensed an era coming to an end. Perhaps he didn't realize that it was more than just the end of his own personal exploration of the Winds. The fur trade was dying, and the railroads were only just getting started on their quest to link up lines in Wyoming. There was to be a fallow period.

"Everything must have an end," Miller lamented as he left one of the temperate stretches of the Winds where he had spent several days hunting, fishing, and painting, "time elapsed, we were in our saddles, and the enchanting scene left as solitary as ever."

Chapter 5

Artists and Manifest Destiny:
Bierstadt and the Surveying Expeditions
(1843-1890)

Sir William Drummond Stewart returned to the Wind River Mountains just four years later, and things had already changed. The Oregon Trail came into significant use in 1836, and by 1846, the hundreds of thousands of settlers venturing west began tamping down the long road, a trail so heavily used that wagon wheels famously wore ruts into the rocky ground. One wagon train alone consisted of nearly 1,000 emigrants, in 1843. That same year, Stewart made the journey west in what is arguably the first pleasure trip to the Winds.

This, Stewart's last trip to Wyoming, did not end well. He brought a large entourage, and threw an elaborate party in which his all-male retinue dressed in velvet and silk Renaissance clothing, on the banks of what is now known as Fremont Lake. A mysterious, trip-ending dispute and evidence of homosexual activities (which were not exactly in vogue at the time) swirl around Stewart's final western tour. Stewart's 1843 trip remains a marker, a clear case of travel in Wyoming for the sake of fun.

The taming of Wyoming (relatively speaking, Wyoming is still plenty wild) was in full swing in 1849 "when an almost unbroken line of wagons stretched across the plains, and for a decade following; it was supposed to be forever set apart as the summer grazing grounds of nature's untamed herds… to be the home of man—never," according to A. S. Mercer, in his self-published 1894 book *The Banditti of the Plains*. But tamed it was—or at least, mapped and assessed by business-minded whites.

It took some adjustment for non-natives from the East. Freight trains in the decade that followed would sometimes trap travelers for the winter, and the oxen pulling the trains had to be let loose to forage in the valleys on their own. "Many a tenderhearted frontiersman was moved almost to tears at the thought of his faithful beasts being left in the wilds as food for wolves," Mercer wrote. "What, then, was their joy when the springtime came and the cattle were found not only to have escaped the fangs of the wolves and mountain lions, but to be fat and sleek, ready for the onward march."

The grasses of the plains, valleys, and foothills were very nutritious. When this revelation spread among whites, the push westward was boosted further. (Not noted yet was the fact that this bounty was dependent on the land not being grazed in the summer—letting the grass grow and go into seed. This was one of many subtleties that were ignored and that subsequently grew into larger problems for white settlers.)

Gold was discovered in Montana in 1859, precipitating problems with Native Americans in the area. Miners flowed into the country driven by gold fever, and the U.S. Army did what it could to make the trails safe for them. But the truces could not withstand the hunger for more land and possible riches supplied by Wyoming's natural resources. By 1864 treaties with the Native Americans were being broken by whites intent on mining and settling, with the U.S. Government usually siding with the settlers. The second Treaty of Fort Laramie offered a withdrawal from Powder River Country of all whites, but for the most part, the white expansion into Native American hunting grounds continued unabated.

Back in 1845, the Democratic Review published an editorial that coined the term "manifest destiny," which pushed the idea that American expansion to the West (aka imperialism) was right and inevitable. The public was divided in regard to this notion, but many politicians, writers, artists, and businessmen in the East fell under the spell of the idea. Manifest destiny didn't merely justify the United States' expansion westward; it also asserted

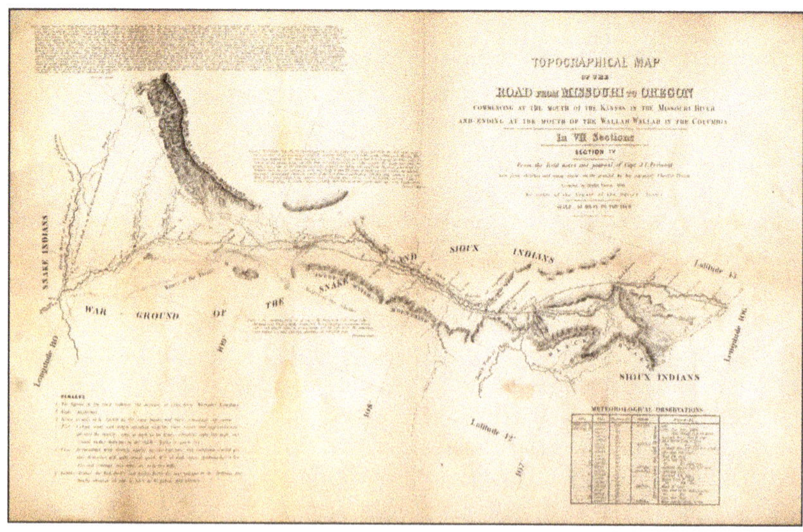

Map of the Oregon Trail.

that the U.S. would serve as a model for other countries. It suggested
American exceptionalism … or perhaps the flip side of the same coin: a bit
of an inferiority complex. Some Americans resented the history, culture, and
perceived superior attitude of Europeans. The supporters of manifest destiny
held that the U.S. would, despite the assumed refinement of nations on the
Continent, serve as the true beacon of ideal governing, profiting, and living,
for the rest of the world. The concept apparently took hold of a German
immigrant from Solingen, near Dusseldorf, and helped inspire him to depict
the grandeur and beauty of America.

Albert Bierstadt was born in 1830,
and his first visit to the American
West was in 1859. Col. Frederick
West Lander invited Bierstadt along

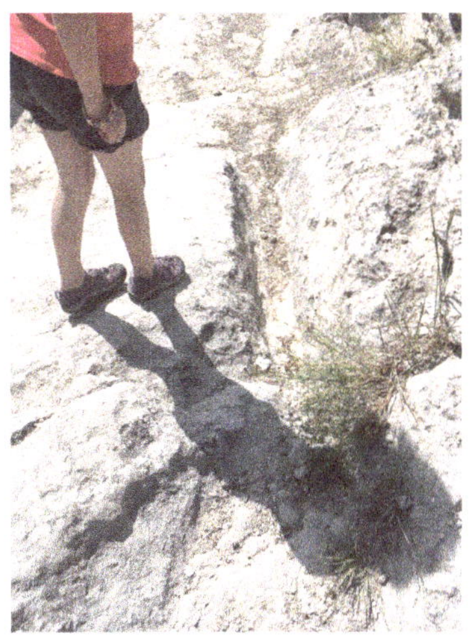

*Top: Wagon wheel tracks dug out in the
rock by the thousands of wagon trains
that made their way along the Oregon
Trail in the mid-1800s. Photo by Amy
Travis.*

*Bottom: Fremont Lake, a favorite spot
of the Scottish explorer Sir William
Drummond Stewart.*

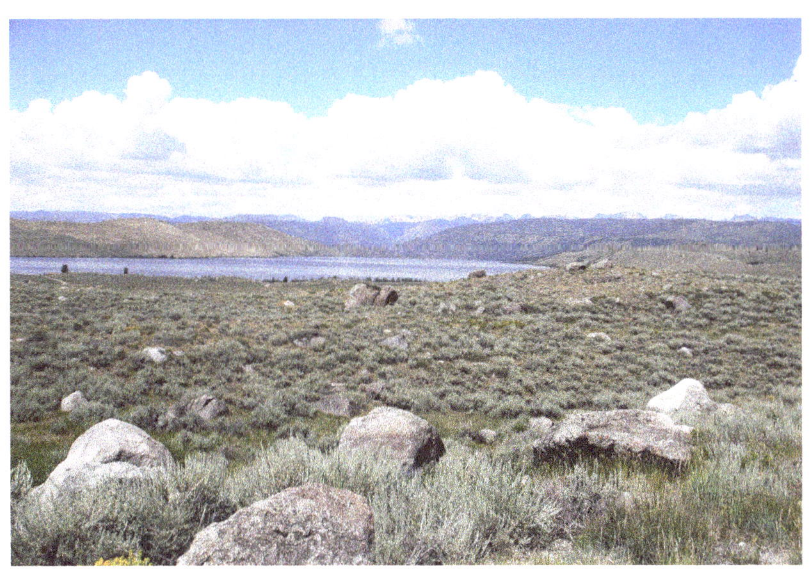

on a surveying expedition to chart a path to Oregon north of the Oregon Trail. At South Pass, Bierstadt went off with a handful of others, six mules, a muleteer, and a spring wagon to explore the Wind River Mountains. This adventure yielded several Bierstadt paintings of note, including "Wind River Mountains—Rocky Mountain Chain" and (completed later in the studio) "Island Lake, Wind River Range, Wyoming" and "The Rocky Mountains, Lander's Peak."

The ambitious and confident German artist had fallen under the spell of Wyoming's ranges of the Rockies. Bierstadt wrote a letter to *The Crayon,* an arts journal, on July 10, 1859, saying "I am delighted with the scenery. The mountains are very fine; as seen from the plains they resemble very much the Bernese Alps…They are of granite formation, the same as the Swiss mountains and their jagged summits, covered with snow and mingling with the clouds, present a scene which every lover of landscape would gaze upon with unqualified delight… The color of the mountains and of the plains, and indeed that of the entire country reminds one of the color of Italy; in fact, we have here the Italy of America in a primitive condition." Bierstadt's quote explains why the concept of manifest destiny is mentioned in regard to American art. Some art historians have gone so far as to label some of the work of Bierstadt and others as "jingoistic," invigorated by a brand of nationalism.

Peter Hassrick, director emeritus of The Buffalo Bill Center of the West, in

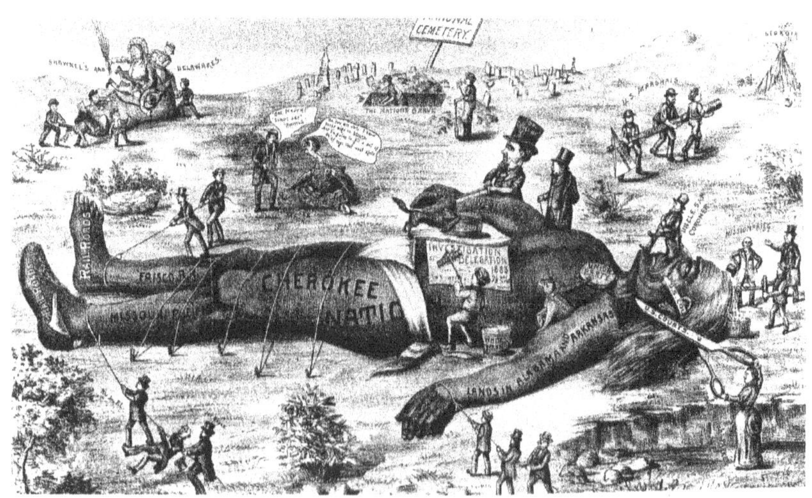

Manifest Destiny cartoon.

Cody, sees a connection with some of the famous New York artists of the day. "Bierstadt and his contemporaries acted as sort of an extension of the Hudson River School mentality, of seeing the grandeur and deific presence in the landscape of the Catskills and Adirondacks," says Hassrick. "But out here, the landscape is even more sublime because it is violent." Indeed, the Tetons don't rise out of the ground. They explode upward. The Winds aren't just majestic. They are utterly wild and difficult to traverse. The Native Americans at that time were still to some degree an impenetrable culture, and there are animals in Wyoming's mountains that would happily eat you. The elements will also kill the unprepared. Bierstadt and his fellow travelers were thrilled with the vigorous experience of the Winds, and were proud this land was part of America. And they were proud of the indigenous people… at this point in history.

"When they say that the Winds are better than Alps, that is a conceit," says Hassrick. "It's another way of self-identifying. At the end of the day, a guy like Alfred Jacob Miller will write in his diary, 'You artists who rush to Europe, who go to France and Italy and paint peasants, could come out here and paint these amazing, unspoiled, uncompromised people who are a genuine American subject. A lot of artists were trying to make these subjects symbols of America.

"The West has been America's future since the 1850s," Hassrick continues. "The trauma of slavery had pushed Americans west. The Compromise of

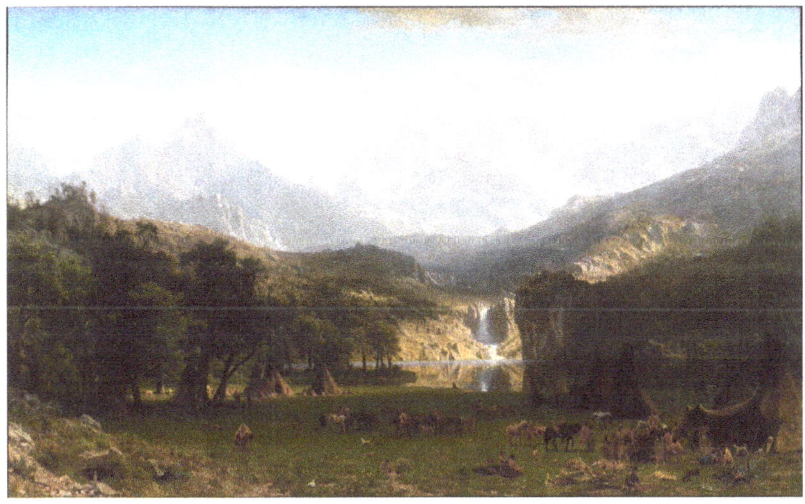

"Landers Peak," by Albert Bierstadt, 1863, oil, 73 ½ x 120 ¾ in.
Collection of the Metropolitan Museum of Art, New York, New York.

1850 divided the West into slavery and nonslavery as a way of avoiding war. The West became a potential salve for the political and social crises that would nearly bring our demise as a country within a decade. The West was a pure world; slavery had not infected it. But it went further; manifest destiny and the divine privilege can be seen in these artists' works. The American identity was wrapped up in the West as theoretically divine sanction of what we deserve. The artists played a role, whether it was conscious or not."

Hassrick recently put together an exhibition titled "Albert Bierstadt: Witness to a Changing West," and one of the ways this title proves true is in the change in the relationship between Native American and non-native people that occurred in Bierstadt's era. Bierstadt arrived in the West when relations were still friendly. "When Bierstadt met the Shoshone it was a mutual admiration society," Hassrick says. "It wasn't until the treaties were violated and the idea grew that the Native Americans were in the way that the big problems started. The Native Americans were left alone when they were not a problem. They became a problem when the army and the government didn't live up to their promises and obligations.

"Yes—when the Rendezvous was in Pinedale, there were some bad players who robbed the mountain men of their harvest and scalped them, leaving them face first in the stream," continues Hassrick. "But most of the tribes at the Rendezvous got along very well with the whites. Read the Lander Expedition journals and Bierstadt's letters back East in 1859 and you'll see their relationship with the Native Americans was very positive. Tribes did not attack wagon trains on the Oregon Trail until the massacres started. Any story that says otherwise was just made up. As soon as the tribes became resistant, they became the bad guy, and that becomes the rationale for taking even more land from them."

Bierstadt seemed to retain a fondness for Native Americans, even as relations soured between the tribes and the whites. His eight-foot canvas "The Last of the Buffalo" was a touching monument to both man and beast. Oglala Lakota painter Arthur Amiotte writes, "Thematically, imagery of Natives in Euro-American art of the 19th Century and early 20th Century has been interpreted by art historians of that period as an homage or tribute to the decline and eventual passing of the American Indian. Their lives were so intrinsically fused with the life of the bison that neither could exist without the other. What Bierstadt perceived and monumentalized in 1888, in his late masterwork, 'The Last of the Buffalo,' focused on the singular act of man heroically and arduously engaged in 'life-threatening competition'

with his prey, the result of which meant continued life for the victor. …
Although the sentiment can be appreciated by non-Native people as a fateful
unfolding of the settling of the West, additional meanings can be gleaned,
perhaps even from the perspective of the American Indian portrayed in the
painting or even, perhaps, from his descendants."

Around 1863 Bierstadt went big, painting canvases as large as 10 feet
across. They were truly grand. "In an outpouring of immense panoramic
canvases, Bierstadt expressed the epic scale of the West by combining
his precise observations of the land with exaggerated, fantastical peaks
dissolving into misty clouds, merging the corporeal with the celestial,"
Laura F. Fry writes in the catalog for "Albert Bierstadt: Witness to a
Changing West." Bierstadt's reputation was international, and substantial.
The critics weren't always kind, but the collectors loved his work, with
one of his last substantial sales, that of "The Last of the Buffalo" to a Col.
North, earning him $50,000—an enormous sum for 1889. Bierstadt's
fortunes fell soon after that, but his place in art history was secured.
"Bierstadt had composed a symphony to America's frontier wilderness
that helped salve national anguish, harmonized nature with the country's
citizens, and promised public liberation through visual travel to a land
beyond most mortal expectations," writes Hassrick. "That is the power his
canvases had, and that is what brought him to the fore as one of the great
picture makers of his day."

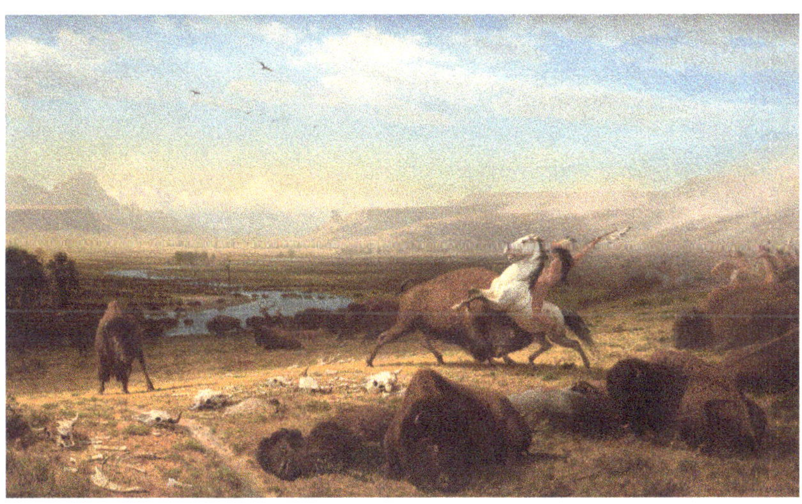

"The Last Buffalo," by Albert Bierstadt,
1888, oil, 30 ¼ x 44 ¼ in. Private collection.

Powerful, yes, but his images are also somewhat romanticized. Even the critics of his day took Bierstadt to task for doing things like putting two waterfalls where there most assuredly was one, and topping off the whole enterprise with a big, bold rainbow. Additionally, Bierstadt almost assuredly didn't even lay eyes on many of the scenes he painted. Art historians have felt sure of this, and they've expressed their doubts going back half a century. In the Metropolitan Museum of Art's publication "The Art Bulletin," Gordon Hendricks wrote in 1964, "There is no evidence that Bierstadt traveled to the Grand Tetons on this trip. Since he was in the Wind River Mountains on July 1, in— and possibly out of—the Wahsatch by July 10, and ready to leave the area, it would have been almost impossible for him to touch

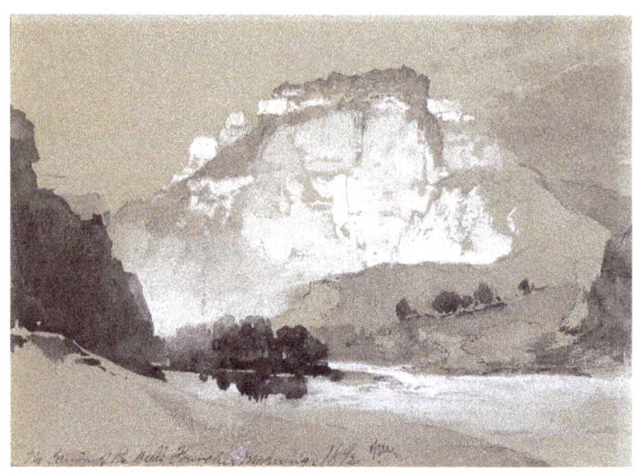

*"Canyon of the Belle Fourche, Wyoming,"
by Thomas Moran, pen, ink, graphite, ink wash,
and white heightening, 7 x 9 1/2 in.*

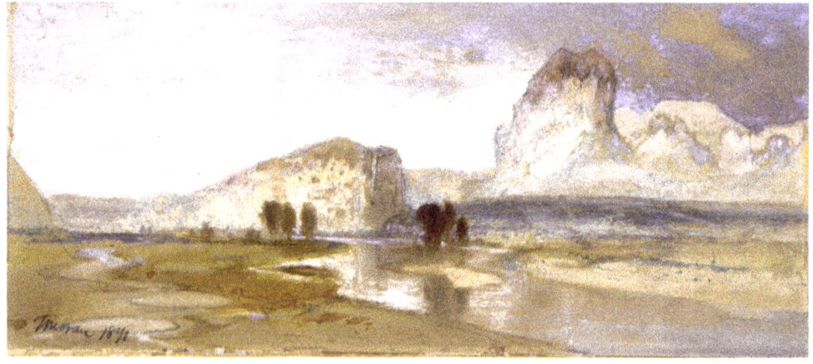

*"First Sketch Made in the West at Green River, Wyoming," by Thomas Moran, 1871,
watercolor, gouache, and graphite on wove paper, 3 ¾ x 8 1/8 in. Collection of the
Gilcrease Museum, Tulsa, Oklahoma.*

the Tetons. The Grand Teton works appear to belong to a nostalgic, reminiscent period of the artist's later life— possibly some time after the Yellowstone trip, when the artist was painting rainbows, waterfalls, etc., into many of his canvases. But I have found no evidence that he was ever in the Tetons: certainly his 'Teton' works do not look like the Tetons."

Bierstadt wasn't unique in this relatively harmless subterfuge. Thomas Moran, born 1837 in Lancashire, England and a U.S. resident from age 7 onward, was commissioned to illustrate an article on Yellowstone National Park for *Scribners* magazine. He worked from descriptions of distinctive landmarks to depict them. In 1871, at the age of 34 but slight and frail, he did go to Yellowstone. Moran's watercolors of the canyon, the lake, the falls, and the photos of Willam H. Jackson, convinced Congress to make Yellowstone a national park in 1872. But Moran never saw the eastern face of the Tetons, even though the 1872 Hayden Survey party honored him with the name Mount Moran.

Thomas Moran diagram of the Badlands of the Yellowstone, 1882.

The visiting artists were a source of amusement for the cowgirls and cowboys of Wyoming. Emma Just recounted her exchange with Moran while he was staying with her family. "I took them into the cellar where I had been churning to give them a drink of fresh buttermilk and while they drank and enjoyed it, I was smoothing the rolls of butter with my cedar paddle that Nels had whittled out for me with his pocket knife," Just wrote in a personal letter. "I noticed the artist man paying special attention to the process and finally he ventured rather apologetically, 'Mrs. Just, would you mind telling me what you varnish your rolls of butter with that gives them such a glossy appearance?' I though the man was making fun of me, or sport

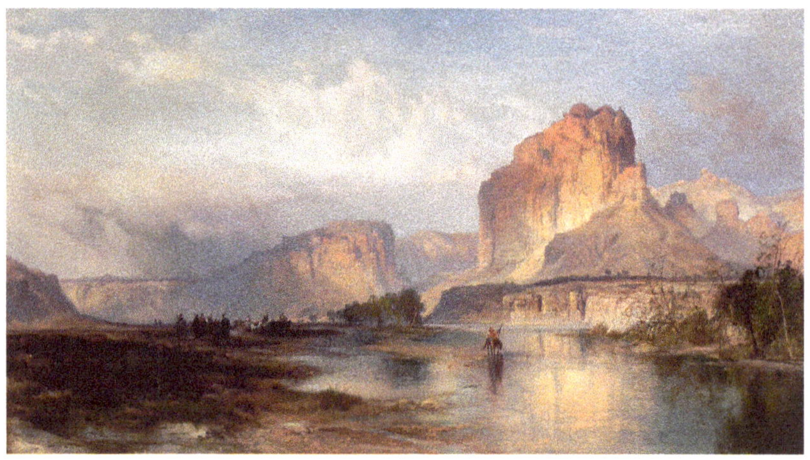

"Cliffs of Green River," by Thomas Moran, oil, 25 x 45 in.
Collection of Amon Carter Museum of American Art, Fort Worth, Texas.

of me as you would express it, but I looked into his face and saw that it was all candor. That is one of the happiest experiences of my life for that man who knows everything to be ignorant in the lines that I know so well. I tried to make him understand that the smooth paddle and the fresh butter were all sufficient but I think he is still rather bewildered. And do you know, since that day, the art of butter making has taken on a new dignity. I keeps singing to me with every stroke, 'Even Thomas Moran cannot do this, Thomas Moran cannot do this,' and before I know it the butter is all finished and I am ready to sing a different song to the washboard."

The Homestead Act of 1862 encouraged more settlers to head west. That act of Congress gave as many as 160 acres of land free to anyone—man, woman, or freed slave—who lived on it for five years and "improved" it. Domestic scenes of butter-making and similar activities were indications of the taming of the Winds, but the mountains were still plenty wild.

In the summer of 1864 Jim Bridger guided a train of about 60 wagons from Casper to Bozeman, MT, his route taking him along the Wind River through Dubois and up to Togwotee Pass. En route, one member of the company, Uhlen, attacked an old man who had outfitted him, and beat him in the head with his own gun. His companions took a vote as to whether to hang him or turn him loose naked and defenseless in the wilderness. The vote was for exile; he was never heard from again.

There was gold along the Wind River, but getting water to it was difficult.

Jeff Standifer took a group of seven men up into the Winds in 1868. They were attacked by Arapahos, and four were killed immediately. One fought from behind a bush and was eventually shot. Another was shot in the thigh. "The Arrapahoes [sic] must have supposed him dead, and Standifer and the man with him having a good position among some rocks nearby, made it so warm for them that they took the horses and left," E. S. Topping wrote. "When the wounded man revived, it was dark, and though all was silent he dragged himself slowly away from the camp. He luckily had a fish line and hooks, and some matches in his pockets, and he concluded to try to get to the Shoshone camp on Little Wind River. He made a rough crutch of a willow fork, and throwing away his gun, started. He struggled and suffered, living solely on fish for eight days; then, just at the mouth of the canyon on Wind River, he met a hunting party of Shoshone, and was taken by them to the main camp, where he was kindly treated until he recovered."

Yank Evarts found himself lost in the Yellowstone area in 1870. He wrote that "his horse ran away from him a few days after he was lost; that when his matches gave out he lighted fires with his glasses (he had left his gun and pistol before), and for the remainder of the trip had to eat his food (fish and thistle roots) uncooked. For the last six or seven days of this terrible time he lived entirely on grasshoppers. He was lost 39 days, and when found weighed just 50 pounds." Later investigations found partially burnt ribs of a horse, suggesting that he ate it and lied about it. News of this ordeal spurred further interest back East.

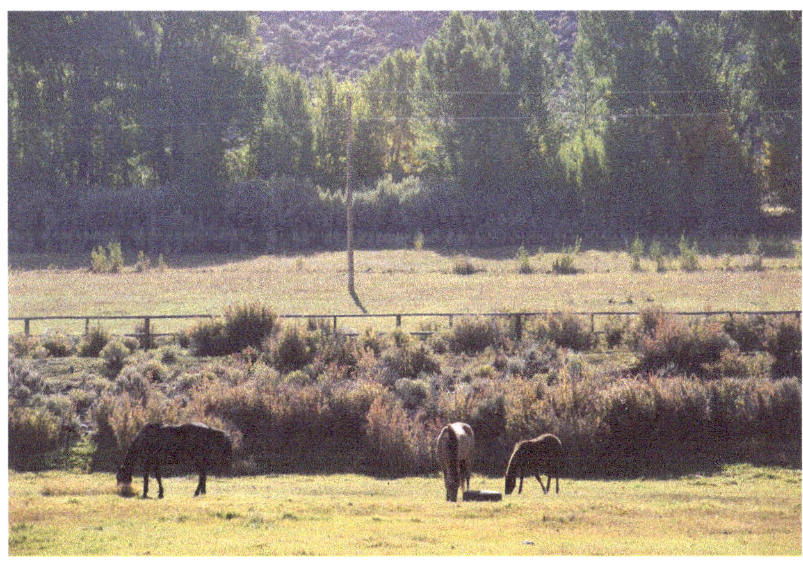

By 1890 the actual Old West was being eclipsed by a new era of ranches, civil order, and rudimentary emergency services. John C. Ewers writes, "So rapidly was the West transformed from unknown Indian country into a settled region that artists had little time to prepare their pictorial record. Within 90 years of the Louisiana Purchase in 1803 the West of the Indian buffalo hunters, of the Rocky Mountain trappers and fort-based Indian traders, the overland trails, the California Gold Rush, the Plains Indian Wars, and the open range of the cowboys had passed into history."

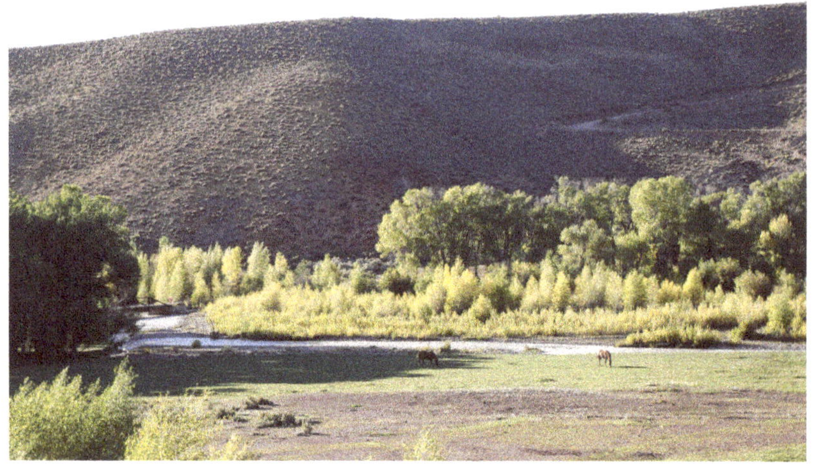

A view at the Finley Ranch, located southeast of Dubois near the start of the Owl Creek Mountains.

Chapter 6

The Modern Era: "My Heart Was in the West" 1890-present

The true nature of the West was being tamed, but it was not disappearing. History was still with the cowboys, for a while. Theodore Roosevelt helped make the rest of the nation aware of the majesty and intoxicating wildness of the West through his magazine articles, books, and widely reported trips. Railroads wanted more passengers, and they took to romanticizing the West further in their pamphlets and posters. And ranches realized money could be made by offering guests—tourists—a taste of the West.

They were called "dude ranches," a term that started out derogatory. A "dude" at the turn of the century referred to a rich man from the East who played at being a cowboy for a while on a working ranch. The name lost its bite over time, at least among the dudes.

One of the first dude ranches was Howard Eaton's place near Medora, in the Dakotas, in the 1880s. He had so many guests staying for as long as several

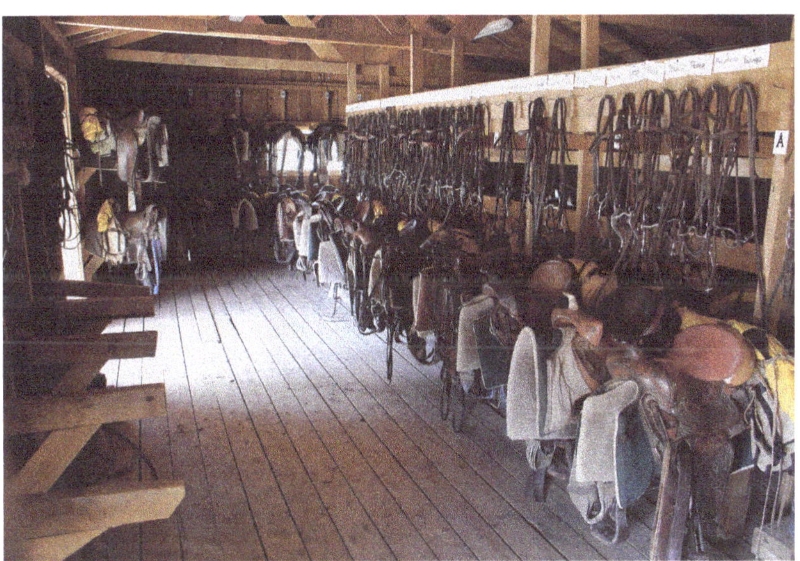

The tack barn at CM Ranch, located near Torrey Canyon.

months that he needed to at least recover expenses from the visitors. This grew into a fee, one that in some years was crucial to the finances of the ranch. Eaton moved his dude ranch to Wolf Creek, outside of Sheridan, Wyoming. The Eaton Ranch is still open for business.

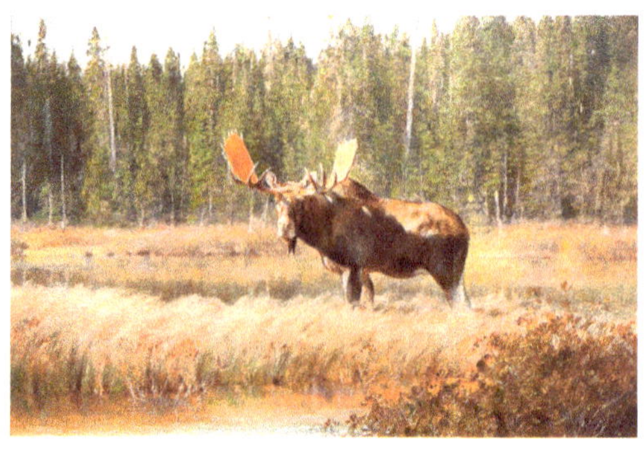

"Bull Moose," by Carl Rungius, oil, 23 ¼ x 35 ½ in. Private collection.

Charlie Moore, the proprietor of CM Ranch, was a leader among dude ranchers, especially in Wyoming. Charlie Moore's father, James K. Moore, was Post Trader for Ft. Washakie, and Chief Washakie himself once reportedly told Charlie that his father, whom they called "Woah," was "the best friend they ever had," according to newspaper reports from the era. Moore and his wife, Marion, ran the CM Ranch near Whiskey Basin, their second go of it. (Moore established a good dude-wrangling business at the mouth of the Dunoir that burned to the ground.) In Arthur Carhart's book *Hi Stranger!*

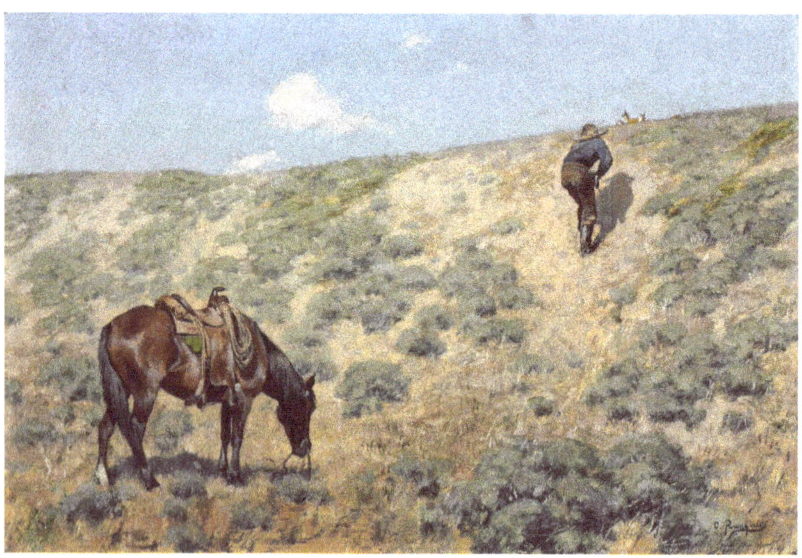

"Hunter Stalking Antelope," by Carl Rungius, oil, 19 ½ x 29 ½ in. Private collection.

The Complete Guide to Dude Ranches, Moore was asked "What started you in the dude business?" His reply: "I wanted to share the life I live." This simple premise allowed dude wranglers the sympathy needed to handle greenhorns. How can you blame the dudes for wanting to live on a ranch for a while?

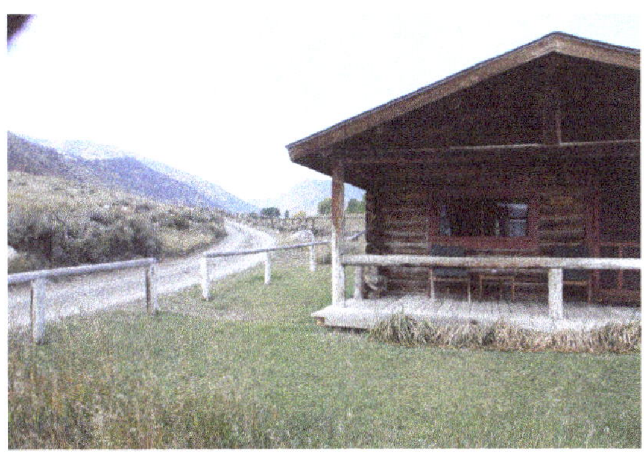

Ogden Pleissner's studio on the CM Ranch.

Moore was a personal friend of both Charles Russell and Frederic Remington. Many dude ranch operators were transplanted Easterners who understood what visitors from the East wanted from a Western experience, but Moore was Wyoming through and through, and he found a way for that to work for him in his business. He was raised on the Wind River Reservation and became annoyed as a young man by his studies at the law school in Michigan, where he learned a profession that he would quickly abandon. His place was on a ranch. Moore was a legendary figure among dude ranch operators, and the CM Ranch remains a favorite destination for tourists looking for a Western vacation.

John Finley's family has run a ranch in the Dubois area for decades, and Finley has worked as a hunting guide and a hand on ranches—both dude and livestock. He explains that a dude ranch requires a fraction of the land that a cattle ranch needs. "Some places of small acreage were dude ranches, but if it were a big ranch, it was just a supplement," Finley says. "They could run dudes and make some extra money. Others bought less land and just ran dudes. But people liked the ones that actually offered cattle drives. There are a few of them still around. People would save up for a while to take a trip—it's not a cheap week of vacation."

Some of the dudes painted. Carl Rungius was an early proponent of Wyoming as inspiration for paintings. He first visited Wyoming in 1895, and he returned nearly every year through 1902, then returning twice more in 1912 and 1915. "I painted from the collected material and later in the spring of 1896, I went back to Germany," Rungius wrote. "My decision to cut all ties with the Old World and to live in America for good was due in no small part to this first Wyoming trip. For my heart was in the West."

Rungius's base of operations in Wyoming was on a ranch outside of Cora. He was such a regular there that one can scarcely call him a "dude." Legends abound regarding Rungius, but one thing is clear: He fully embraced the Western aesthetic. He was the top big-game wildlife artist of his time and one of the enduring great painters of the Rocky Mountains. Later, he focused on the Canadian Rockies, growing to love the area around Banff, in Alberta. His ashes were distributed on Tunnel Mountain after his death in 1959. "Wyoming still has elk and antelope and mule deer; sagebrush prairies, and mountains that flame up and glow deep blue and purple when the day dies; friendly people who welcome strangers. But part of her is lost, never to be regained—that indefinable something that might be termed, for want of a better name, the Spirit of the Old West," writes William J. Schaldach in *Carl Rungius, Big Game Painter.* "It stirs the imagination of everyone who loves America; it is among our finest traditions. Carl Rungius was fortunate in being able to drink a last long draught before the stream dried up forever."

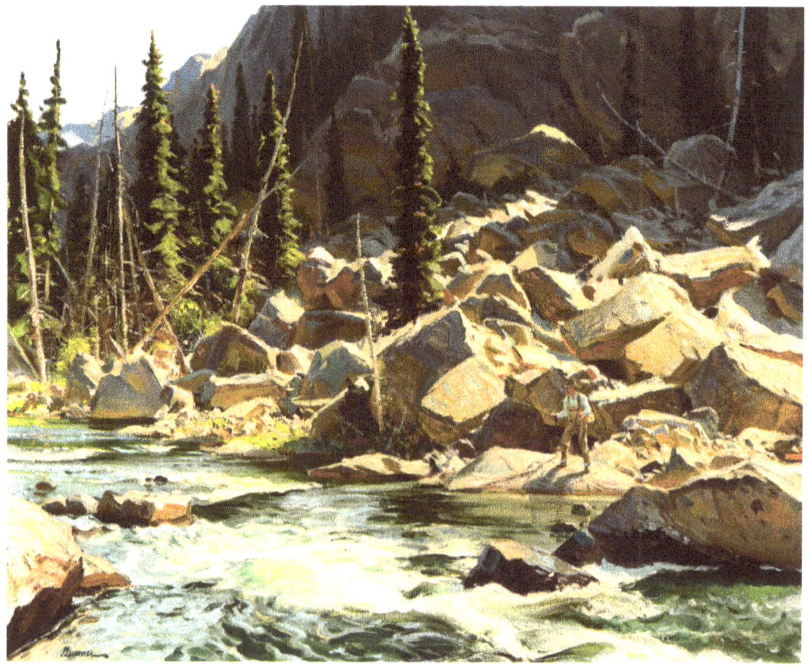

"Fishing the Headwaters of the Wind River,"
by Ogden Pleissner, oil, 24 x 30 in. Private collection.

Historian Struthers Burt asserts that the dude ranch biz, which hit its height in the 1930s, was inevitable. "The dude business is a bona fide business," he wrote. "…The demand was there before the supply. The demand had been growing in a tentative sort of way ever since the 1870s and the time when it became possible for the first dudes to reach the West without much danger of being scalped. Americans young and old want to go to ranches. And they want to live on ranches. And they want to do what people do on ranches."

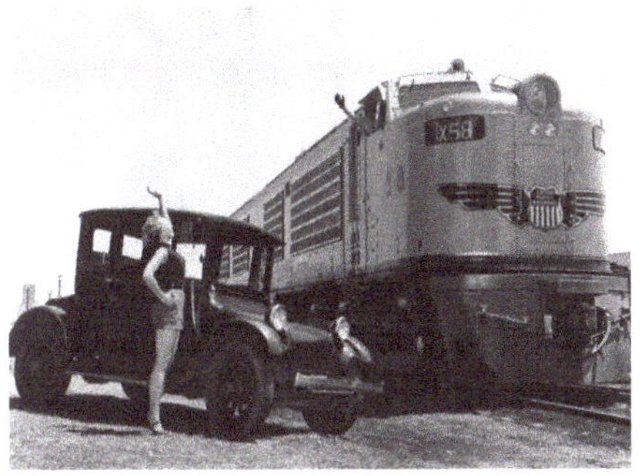
Union Pacific diesel.

And some people want to paint. Ogden Pleissner became acquainted with the Wind River Mountains at the age of 16; he spent several summers as a youth in the Dubois area. From 1921 through the 1950s Pleissner visited Wyoming often, staying at the CM Ranch so frequently that a cabin with a view of Jakey's Fork was set up as a studio for him on the premises. His watercolors depicting sporting scenes, appearing in outdoor magazines and other publications, helped stoke interest back East for the Wind River

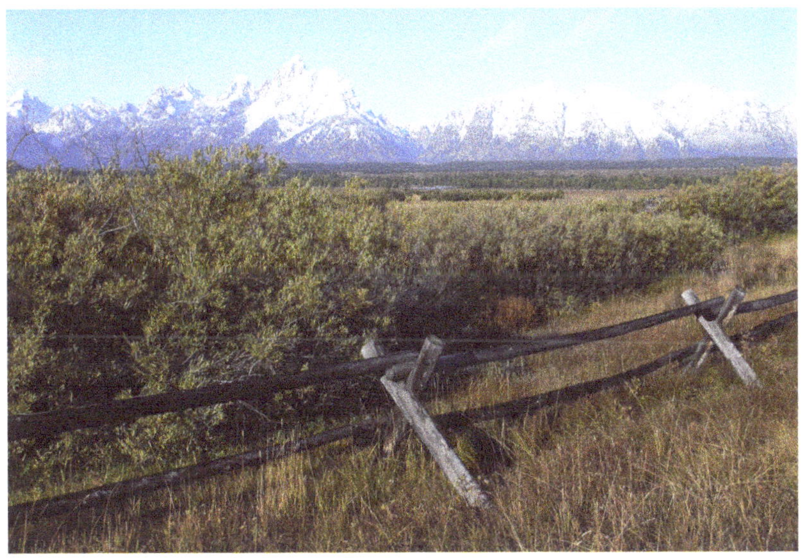
Buck-and-rail fence.

lifestyle. Was he painting the Old West? No, but he was painting the wildness that still lived in Wyoming, and his paintings vibrate with this idyllic vitality.

Famous Regionalist painter Thomas Hart Benton vacationed and painted in the Winds. Others, less famous, ventured west as well. Such as West— Levon West. This draftsman made etchings and drypoint drawings that impressed even the skeptical dude wranglers running the ranches. The February 1935 issue of *The Dude Rancher,* the trade publication for dude wrangling, wrote about West's exhibition of drawings and watercolors in Boston and New York. "There is more and more of this sort of thing, of the slouching grace of the long-legged cowboys lolling or standing in their stirrups to howl into line an errant colt," the account reads. "Mr. West delights in the sharp characteristic lines of bridles and gear, he understands the structure of horses and paints them swiftly with a brush too familiar with their svelte flanks to put down any but eloquent symbols. All those who have known the life of the West and those who understand the loneliness, the hard work on the ranges, and the faithful companionship of patient horses will appreciate in Mr. West's work his sincerity, simplicity, and lack of pose."

The dude ranches had a powerful ally in the railroad companies, which were interested in boosting ridership on their trains running through this

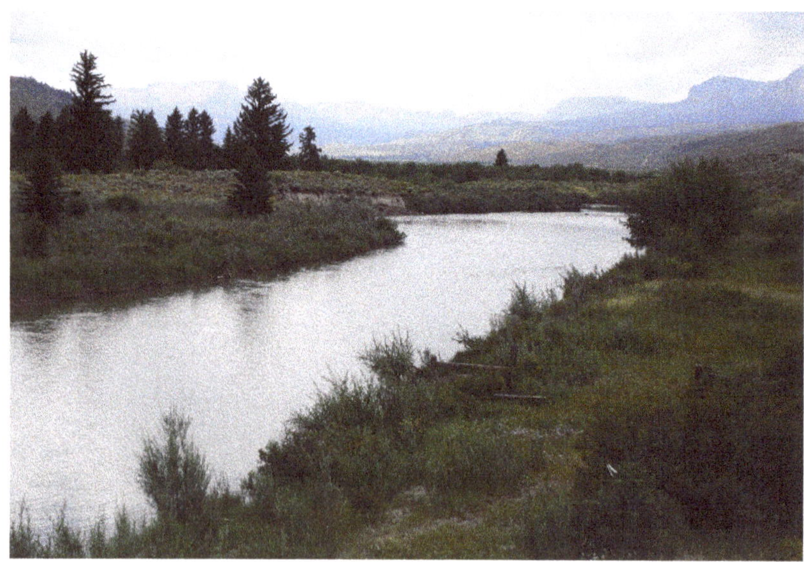

The spot where Dunoir Creek enters the Wind River.

wild land. An article by W. S. Basinger, passenger traffic manager of the Union Pacific, in the April 1937 issue of *The Dude Rancher,* states, "In the interest of dude ranches along its lines, the Union Pacific is conducting an advertising and selling campaign to promote dude ranch vacations. Backing up our advertising is a sales force of general agents and representatives keenly interested in this dude business. From our headquarters at Omaha an intensive direct mail campaign is also waged. We are using attractive window displays through the East to invite the dudes' attention to our attractive booklet called 'Dude Ranches'—this book is rated by the ranchers themselves as 'tops' in the field, and it really sells the dudes. This common heritage has brought the ranchers and the railroad closer together in a mutual endeavor to provide genuine American vacations."

The railroad made the Oregon Trail seem outdated. The Union Pacific railroad, with the blessing of the federal government, identified the 41st Parallel as the optimal path for a railroad track across Wyoming.

When the Union Pacific worked its way across the state and reached Utah in 1868, it left Wyoming changed. The railroad industry had immense sway in government in Wyoming, centered on its large land grants and the taxes it paid that enriched local coffers. As the railroad was built across the state, the workers looked for fun ways to spend their pay. Cheyenne and Laramie became party towns…but only so long as the railroad was being built and the construction continued to infuse cash at the pointed tip of the railroad's expansion. As the rails were completed, the workers moved on, as did the party.

For the towns that experienced the railroad being built, the boom soon busted, but the railroad's impact was only beginning. Ranchers could much more easily send their stock to auction. Industry was possible, with trains available to ship products made with Wyoming natural resources to cities beyond the borders. People had a way to make a living in the High Plains, a dry, windy landscape so tough to work that fences were almost always buck-and-rail. A buck-and-rail fence does not require digging holes in the rocky ground for posts. The "buck" part of the fence is the X-shaped construction every several feet, with the rails running parallel to the ground and nailed to the bottom sections of the X. The fences are now considered as beautiful as they are practical, but the lodgepole pines often used for the buck-and-rail fences were soon to help also build structures with a much greater level of craftsmanship and beauty, as we will see.

Even without any human structures, northwest Wyoming is, obviously, breathtaking. The dude wranglers understood this and were on the frontlines of conservation. "There are going to be attempts to make inroads into the primitive areas and we must stand firm in the future in our protection of these areas," said Col. Allen Peck, regional forester based in Denver, when he spoke to the Dude Ranchers' Association seventh annual meeting in Livingston, Montana, on October 27, 1932. Adds Struthers Burt, "Beauty has been proven to be a business asset, game need never disappear, neither need an intelligently controlled and restricted wilderness, and tourists have been shown to be the biggest future the high sections of the Rocky Mountain States have." *The Sheridan Press* said in 1933, "The dude wranglers have done a good job with their industry. If they had not from the very beginning been single-minded in conserving and not exploiting this gorgeous country—if they had not been determined to make their appeal to only the finest sportsmen and real outdoor lovers of the East—if they had not stood together in keeping the spirit of the West alive, recreation in the Rocky Mountains might easily have degenerated into a cross between Coney Island and a honky-tonk."

One can easily imagine a conversation between two white men in the early days of white expansion into the Winds. What did they see, looking down the Wind River from the headwaters above Dubois? Arable land doesn't open up until one heads further east in the Wind River Valley, and even

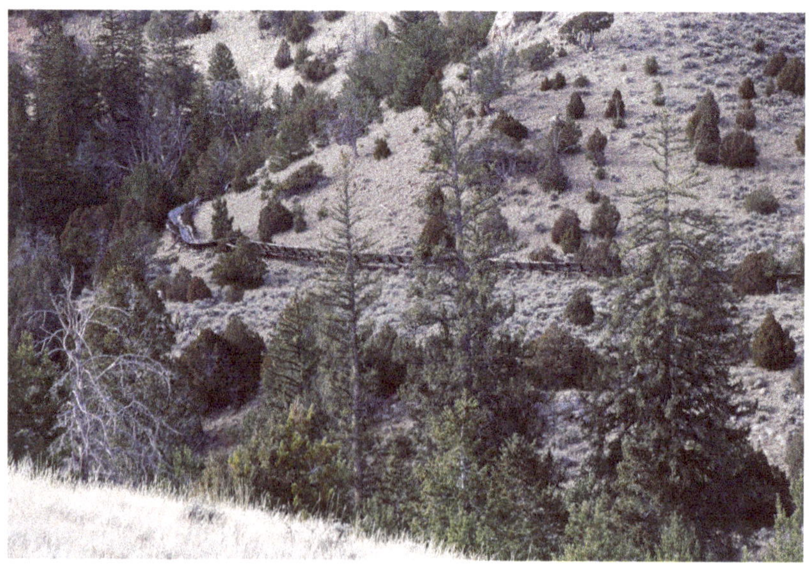

Tie flume.

then, it is not ideal farmland. It didn't look promising for grazing cattle, either, although ranchers soon learned the cows knew how to find food on the hills. There was plenty of game, but plenty more steep cliffs, rocky hills, and dense pine. As dude rancher and artist Joe Back wrote in his short story "Shoshoni Pass," "If you don't believe this here park county of Wyoming is about the straight uppest and vertical downest country in the Rocky Mountain section of Wyoming to guide and hunt in, I'll put in with you. Maybe you've been there; if you have, I'll bet you never forget it. When you're not going up, you sure are goin' down!"

But the pine-covered Winds offered timber, and the Wind River offered a way to transport the logs downstream nearly 100 miles to Riverton, from thence they could hop a freight and be delivered wherever needed. The question

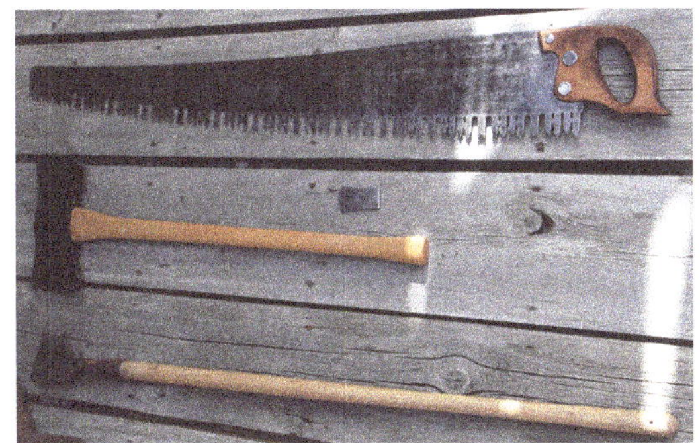

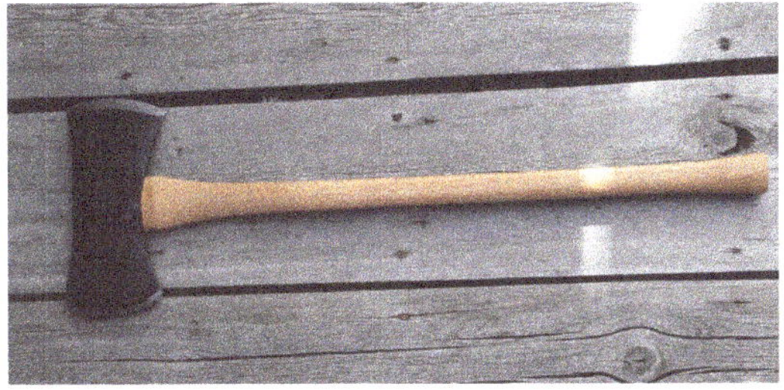

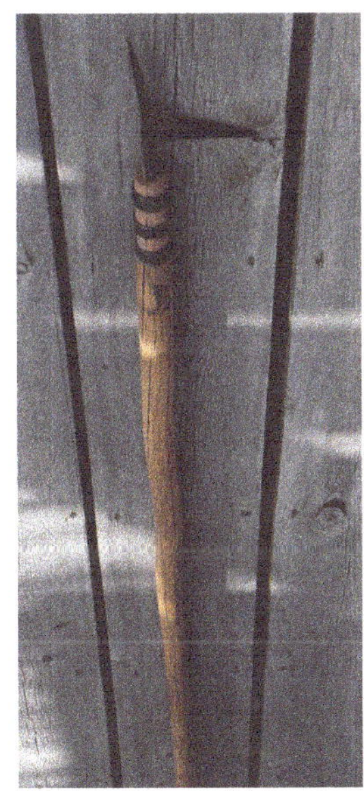

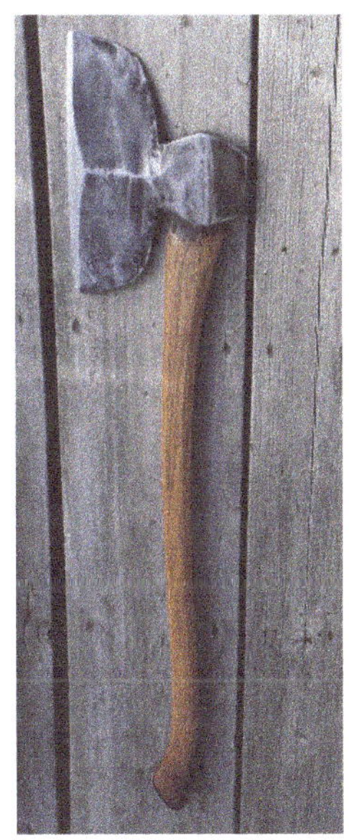

Tie hack tools.
Top: saw, axe, chisel
Middle: two-sided axe
Bottom: pike and broad axe

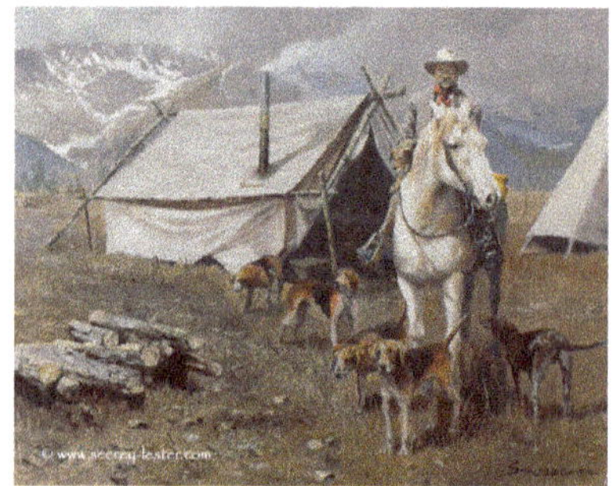

"TR & Skip Headin' Out,"
by John Seerey-Lester, oil, 16 x 20 in.

was how to get the lodgepole pines off the mountain and onto the Wind River so they could float down with the snowmelt-driven current in late spring. The answer to this problem required two things: manpower and innovative thinking. The manpower was solved by hiring immigrants from Scandinavia. And the innovation came via tie flumes, which were in use elsewhere, but had to be dramatically re-engineered for the 2,000-foot canyons the timber companies were facing in the Winds.

Ties are the horizontal, spaced logs that lay under the rails on railroad tracks. Tory Taylor recalls Back telling him, "Ties were hewn, or hacked, by men using only hand tools. Green pine trees were felled with a crosscut saw, limbed with double-bitted ax, squared on two sides to an eight-inch-thickness, and finally cut into eight-foot lengths. The ties, often weighing up to 200 pounds, were then tossed upon the broad shoulder of the tie hack and carried to the nearest wagon, road, or stream for future transportation. Then the tie hack would spin on his heel and go do it again—up to 50 times a day."

The railroad's expansion west required an enormous amount of railroad ties—as many as 2,800 were needed for every mile of track. Each tie was eight feet long, with a 7 ¾" depth and an 8-10" width. A tie hack could get as many as five ties out of a good-size tree. They were paid by the tie; they notched the end of each tie with their personal mark. The pay was 10 cents a tie at first, 30 cents by the 1930s, and 50 cents at the end of the tie-hack era, in the mid to late 1940s. The woods boss of the Wyoming Tie & Timber Company, Martin Olson, grew up in Namsos, Norway, and he successfully recruited woodsmen from Norway and Sweden. The tie hacks made 12 times as much doing the work in Wyoming than they would have made in Scandinavia, according to Mark Goodman, an author and an old tie hack. Tie hacks manufactured between 15 and 30 ties a day, making as much as $9 per day—a nice rate for the time.

The ties were made by cutting down a lodgepole pine—an evergreen with a particularly straight and perfectly tapered trunk—using a crosscut saw that was wielded by a hack and occasionally manned by two tie hacks. (Spruces were also sometimes harvested.) The tie hack would then walk along on top of the trunk, removing limbs with a double-bit ax, which has a blade on either side—one heavy and blunter, the other razor sharp. The tie hack would take the sharp side to start peeling off one side of the

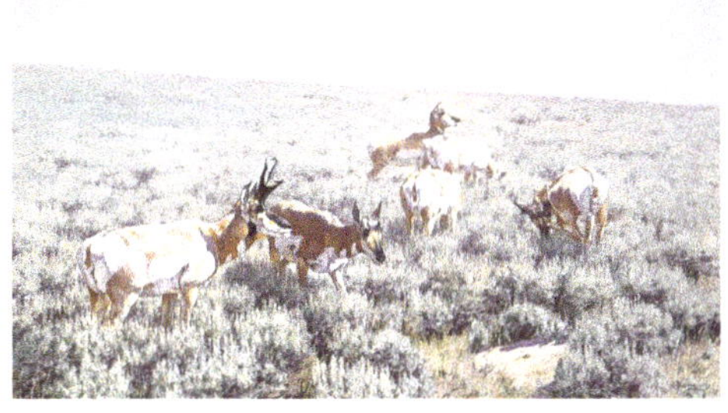

"Wyoming Sage," by Carl Rungius, 1902, oil.

tie to get a flat surface. The other side of the tie was then started by biting into the log in similar fashion. Next came the broadax, with its nine-pound head and 12" blade. The broadax allowed the tie hack to make the two sides uniformly flat. When a tie hack finished with the two flat surfaces, they were so smooth the surfaces seemed planed. A spud peeler—a long-handled tool with a curved blade at the end—was then used to pull off the bark from the two uncut sides. Finished ties were then stacked and made ready for one-ton draft horses to drag the ties away.

That's when the tie flume came into the picture.

During World War I, the government had control of railroads, and contracts for replacement ties were largely curtailed. In addition, the easily harvested

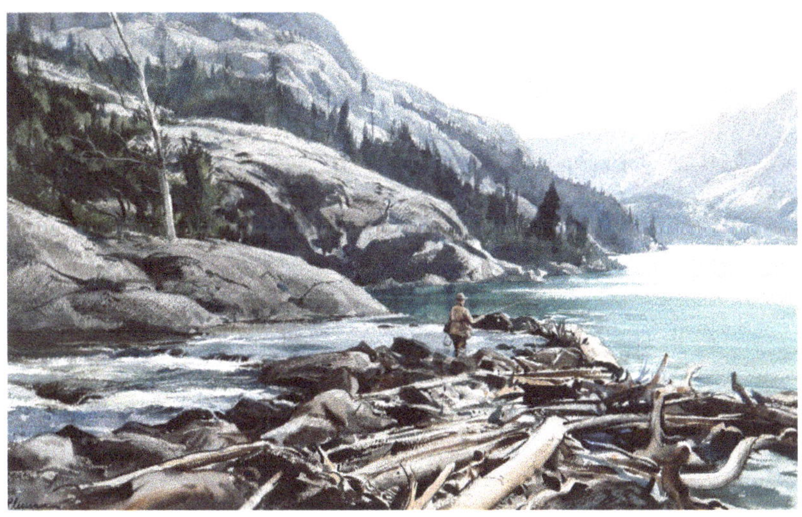

"The Outlet—Ross Lake, Wyoming," by Ogden Pleissner, watercolor, 16 x 25 ½ in.

timber along the upper Wind River Valley was gone, requiring Olson to look higher in the Wind River Mountains for good stands of trees. He found an enormous reservoir high up above Warm Springs Creek Canyon. The challenge was getting the cut ties down the mountain and onto the Wind River. Olson had several years to figure it out. When the railroads were released from government control in 1921, the issue became more urgent, as the demand for railroad ties went up again. But even building a road to Olson's envisioned camp high up on the mountain was considered impossible by road engineers. He responded by hiring a bulldozer operator and bulldozing the "impossible" road grade by walking in front of the dozer and showing him the path he had in mind. Olson was ready to do what some said couldn't be done.

Olson had a vision, dating back to 1918, of how the flume could be built, and where. He hired an engineering firm from Seattle to take control of the actual construction, but the flume's placement and path were all Olson. Work began in 1926. The engineers presented problems that were seemingly insurmountable, and Olson countered with ideas. In one passage of the flume, it was suspended by cables from above to secure it. In another, it went through a natural cave. The grade at times was about 45 degrees—so steep that if they didn't shoot water down the flume along with the ties, the ties (traveling at 50mph) caught on fire.

The Warm Springs Canyon flume was indeed built, and it allowed the Wyoming Tie & Timber Company to flourish. Some accounts assert that as many as 10 million ties were cut and transported by the company from 1914 to the mid-1940s, when demand for ties dropped off and portable sawmills became financially advantageous. That number is suspiciously round, however.

The story is plenty interesting enough without any exaggeration. The tie hack life was, quite simply, epic. They were largely on their own. The men were pointed to a stretch of evergreens, about a half-mile long and about 200 feet wide, and told it was theirs to cut. The tie hacks were paid by the piece--based on what they actually cut.

If a tie hack was getting stir crazy up on the mountain, he could blow off work, head to the Rustic Pine Tavern in Dubois, and go on a bender, drinking as much as he could afford. The men called it being "off on a toot." If someone were away for too long, Olson would send word for him to return. If the carouser ran out of money, he could call Olson for an extension on his pay, and Olson would often acquiesce, with the understanding that

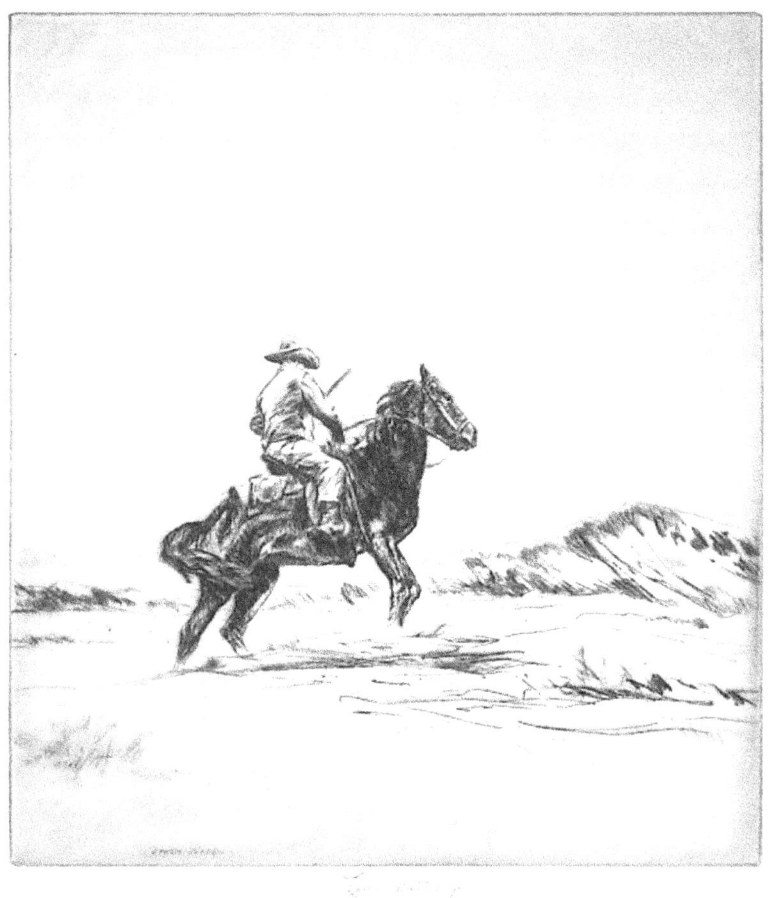

"The Prairie Rider," by Levon West, 1933, drypoint, 8 ½ x 7 ¾ in.

the tie hack needed to get it out of his system and get back to work soon.

They were prodigious eaters, workers, drinkers, and brawlers. It was a life hard-lived. Often, workers would carouse in Dubois and just get back to their tents on the mountain after midnight. If they didn't get up the next morning, their tent was collapsed on them and they were kneed as punishment. Thenceforth, carousing appeared slightly less appealing.

Olson and his fellow Scandinavians felt somewhat at home in the Winds. They understood the alpine nature of their new residence. It's a good thing, too—the tie hacks were snowed-in high in the mountains for as long as three months a year. Luckily, they knew how to ski from their time back in the Old Country. But Joan Trego Pinkerton writes that in Wyoming, they had to ski to and from work on less than Olympic-level equipment.

"'Boards' is the apt description for those early-day skis. Most of them were homemade and bore little resemblance to today's sleek, narrow cross-country counterparts. The skis were wider and much longer, and of course were made entirely of wood, since plastic hadn't yet been invented. Various methods were employed to assist the skier in moving uphill, such as animal skins strapped on the bottom of the boards so the fur gripped the snow while climbing. The men seldom used a set of poles. Usually they had just one very long pole used for balance and to act as a brake on steep slopes. When they wanted to slow down, they just straddled the pole and sat back."

A modern reader may wonder how much of all this is pure exaggeration. To be sure, this was still the West, where storytelling was a respected skill. Consider the tale of a tie hack named Big Thor, who was challenged during a toot to a cutting duel over one month's time. At the end of the month, he returned to the saloon and bought drinks all around, and announced that he had cut more than 2,000 ties, an average of 70 a day. "The challenger gulped down his drink and hurriedly left without revealing his record," according to an Associated Press story.

There's no sugar-coating it; the tie hacks were largely very hard drinkers. Legend is that because there was no dentist, both the toothache sufferer and the amateur dentist (a fellow tie hack) fortified themselves with whiskey before attempting to pull the offending tooth, occasionally resulting in more than one tooth being pulled, including—hopefully—the tooth responsible for the pain. "Many of the men ended up with few, if any, of their own teeth over the years and eventually had to send to the big city for a set of artificial choppers, having first made crude wax impressions of their own jaws," Pinkerton writes in *Knights of the Broadax*. "The mail-order plates were seldom comfortable, and they seemed to get in the way, particularly during a drinking spree, so they would be taken out and often mislaid. The next morning after a bash would find the woolly-headed men passing around sets of teeth to 'try out' to see if they fit well enough to be claimed."

They fished, mostly for trout, with a few whitefish sneaking onto their stringers. They hunted—elk, deer, and occasionally bear, but not moose. Moose were "the undisputed monarchs of the woods," according to Pinkerton. She tells an anecdote helping to explain why. "One winter day,

Johnson didn't show up for dinner and was found later standing atop a pile of ties, just out of reach of a testy moose pacing around the stack," writes Pinkerton. "The searchers shooed the animal away, and a relieved Johnson came down from his perch to eat a cold supper."

Without the Warm Springs Canyon Flume, few tie hacks would have been needed, and the Upper Wind River Valley would have "developed" much more slowly. The timber operation infused the area with cash and people—although Dubois still prides itself on being "high in altitude, low in multitudes." The flume itself is a beautiful piece of craftsmanship, without the symbolic importance assigned to functional Native American craftsmanship … maybe it simply symbolizes the arrival of capitalism and white civilization, ideas that continue to have the greatest impact on Wyoming.

But is it art?

The flume is an M-shaped structure, five feet wide at the top, generally made of 2'x4's. The ties shoot down the flume in the V-part of the M. A telephone line ran along the Warm Springs Canyon flume, in large part to allow for communication should there be a problem and the flow needed to halt. When a break happened in the flume, they would telephone the top to

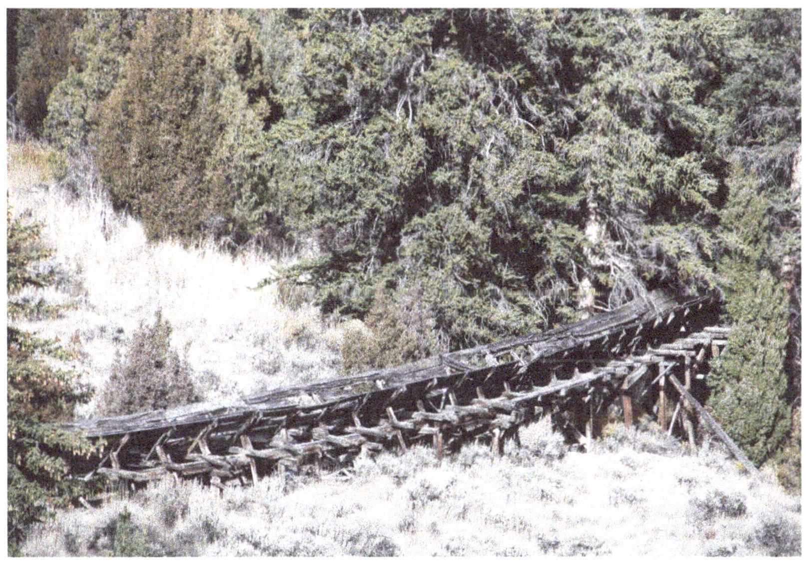

The flume, an engineering feat that inspired art.

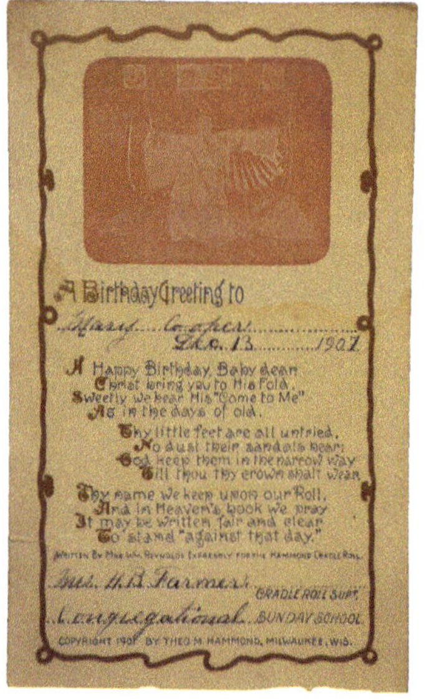

Mary Back's birth certificate.

stop the flow of logs. One break resulted in more than 1,500 ties falling into the canyon. They had to be dragged back up to the flume by hand.

Materials to continue building the flume were sent down…via the flume. In the fall of 1928, after 10 years of Olson walking the mountains and forming his design, and after one year of building his creation, the Warm Springs Canyon tie flume was finished, with its mouth feeding the larger flume that carried ties to the Wind River. The local newspaper, the *Courier Dubois,* reported on the celebration upon its completion. Robert and Elizabeth Rosenberg, two Wyoming historians, write, "Finally, the Warm Spring Canyon tie flume was complete. After months of hard labor in the steep canyon, workers of the Wyoming Tie and Timber Company and some 250 guests celebrated in November 1928 at a banquet-dance in the DuNoir tie camp, high in the Wind River Mountains. At five o'clock dinner was served in the large mess hall. 'Long tables the full length of the room fairly groaned under their heavy load of fried chicken, veal, salads, oyster dressing, biscuits, sauces, and many more good things to eat,' the local *Courier Dubois* reported. "Paddy's Jazz Kings of Riverton took the stage after the tables were cleared, and the dancing began. After a midnight lunch, couples danced until the sun came up. Flapjacks and country sausage were served for breakfast and the guests found their weary ways to bed."

World War II nearly killed off the tie business in the Winds. Everything went to the war effort, and the men were needed in the military. But the war soon provided its own answer: prisoners of war from Germany. Yes, it was forced labor. But compared to the various alternatives, physical work outdoors in beautiful country with extremely well-prepared food three meals a day was a decent option. Contemporary accounts get a little carried away, quoting P.O.W.'s saying things such as "What a way to spend the war!" and asserting that minimal guarding of the enemy prisoners was sufficient because they loved the work so much. More than likely, the Germans couldn't see an easy way out. Regardless, they worked alongside the tie hacks and acquitted themselves well.

By the end of the war, mobile engines were much more common, and thus so were portable sawmills. Trucks replaced horses, and construction equipment was improved. The tie hacks were quickly rendered obsolete. The increased efficiency had its price, however. "The forests used by the tie hacks were very selectively cut," Joe Back wrote. "A tree had to be just the right size and age to be suitable for making railroad ties. … The tie hacks cultivated the forests as carefully as a gardener would weed a row of table vegetables. Today many areas logged by the light on the land methods of tie hacking are eligible for wilderness designation, a sharp contrast to the denuded land often left behind by mechanized logging." Martin Olson, general manger of the Wyoming Tie & Timber Company, visited a modern logging operation in the Winds when he was well into his retirement. He left crying.

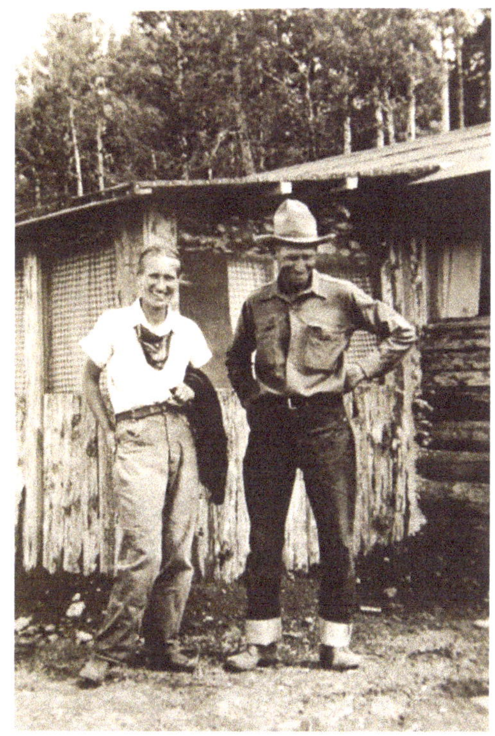

Mary and Joe Back.

The flume is still there, mostly. It's been hit with weather, vandalized, suffered from disrepair. It's completely in ruins in several places. But enough of the structure is still visible to see its beauty. But, again, is it art?

"It's certainly an engineering feat, which could be an art form in a way," says John Finley, a lifetime Dubois resident, rancher, and local historian. "Art shows won't accept functional art, so they won't accept a saddle because it is functional, although it is definitely artistic, even though it has been tooled. It's the same with pottery and ceramics, although the guild here has accepted some as art. The flumes have definitely inspired art. There are plenty of drawings of the flume, and I'm sure there are paintings done of them, too. If the flumes are not art, they have certainly inspired art."

The tie hack business was undone by automation, which was goosed by the necessities of World War II. That war brought changes to other parts of the Wind River economy as well. Further up the Wind River Valley, up closer to Togwotee Pass, Joe Back and his wife, Mary, faced a decision in 1941.

Mary Back was born Mary Waters Cooper in 1906 in Minneapolis. Her parents moved Mary and her three siblings to Rutland, Vermont shortly thereafter. Mary grew up appreciating the outdoors, and her familiarity with outdoor life and a dexterity working with her hands increased with her attendance at Berea College, a quirky, rustic Kentucky institution located in the Appalachian Mountains that has free tuition but the requirement of work service. At Berea, Mary sharpened her skills in woodworking, and learned more about traditional crafts.

She was accepted into the Art Institute of Chicago in 1928 and found herself swept into painting and drawing animals of all kinds. Mary served as an intern at the Field Museum of Natural History, placing her in classes such as "animal structure," and creating scenarios in which Mary found herself raising mice, and maybe taking a live snake home on the elevated train so she could sketch it. She met with luminaries such as

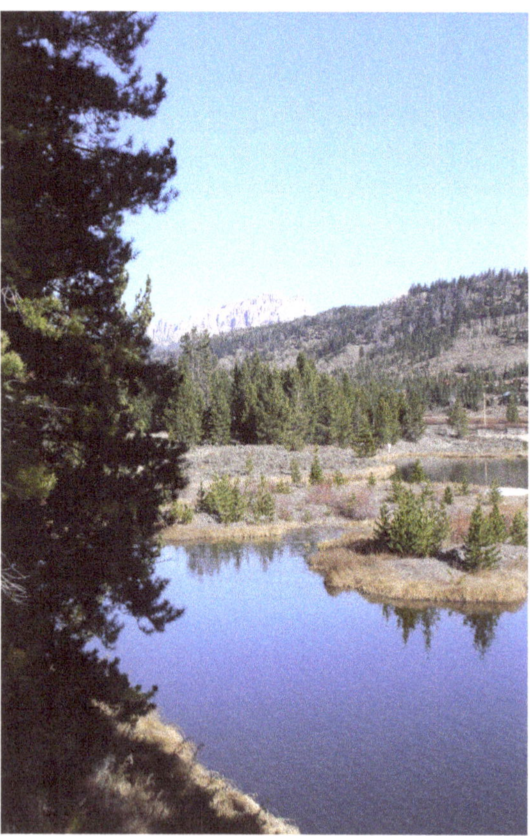

The view from the Back's house at the Lava Creek Ranch.

Charles R. Knight, the famed muralist who painted prehistoric and other natural scenes in museums across the country. She would later look back on her college years and her stay in Chicago as the happiest time of her life.

Mary was sketching a bear in the Field Museum one day for her animal anatomy class when she was interrupted by a visitor. "Suddenly a loud voice boomed over her shoulder, 'That's a hell of a bear!'" Ruth Mary Lamb writes in her excellent book *Mary's Way: A Memoir of the Life of Mary Cooper Back.* "Mary turned and froze the loud stranger with an angry stare, muttering to herself about the 'damn tourists.' Before her stood a roughly handsome young man with sparkling blue eyes, who decided pretty quickly that Mary Cooper was someone he wanted to get to know better."

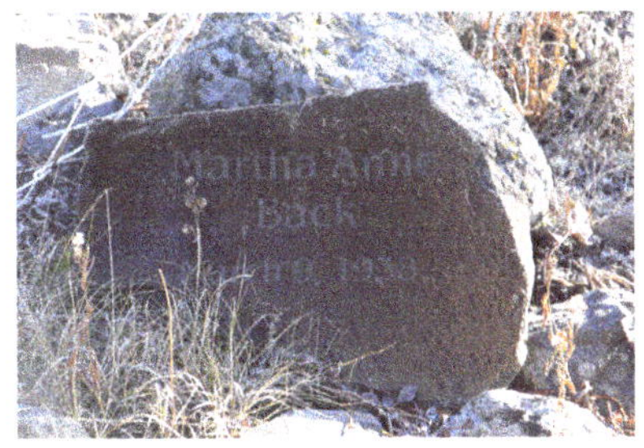

Mary did what any sensible young woman would do in such a situation: She named her pet crow after him. Then she married him. His name was Joe Back.

Back was in the Navy during World War I, and afterward worked as a ranch hand at various places in Wyoming. While he was working on a dude ranch outside of Dubois, one of the guests was Louis Agassiz

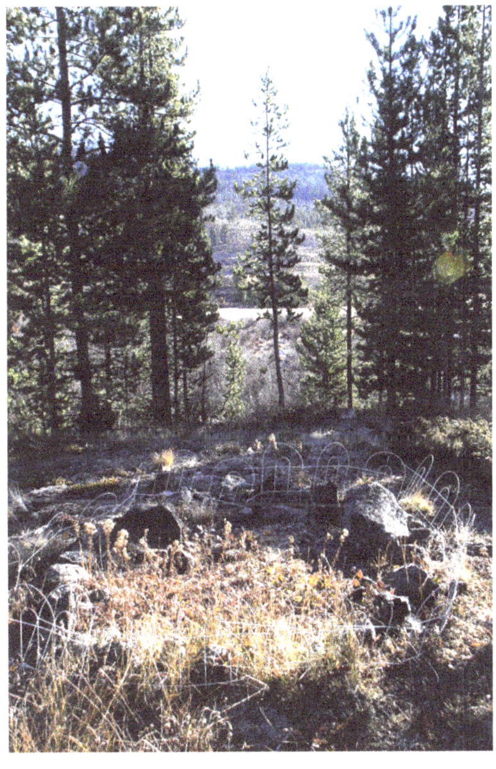

The grave marker and gravesite of Martha Anne, the daughter the Backs lost in childbirth. The site is carefully maintained by the current owner.

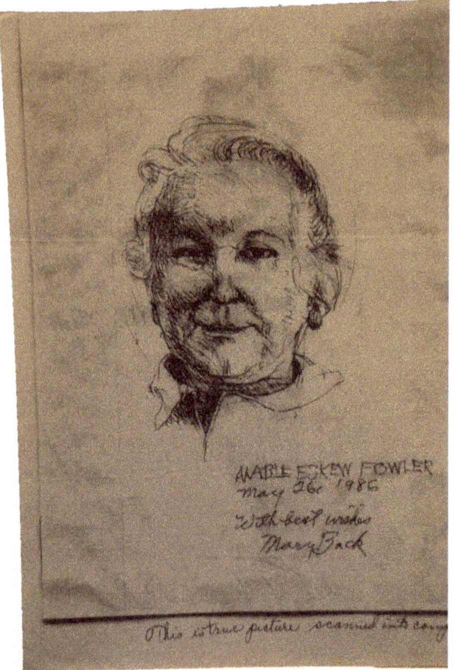

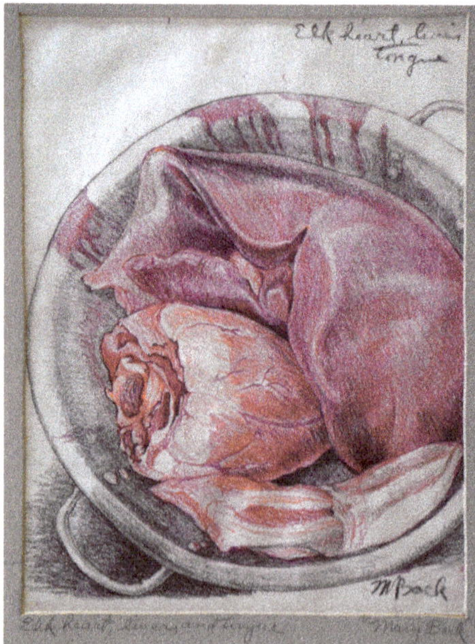

An impromptu sketch (top) and a drawing of an elk heart (bottom) by Mary Back.

Fuertes, an accomplished illustrator and ornithologist. Fuertes saw some of Joe's drawings, and urged him to apply to the Art Institute of Chicago. They turned him down because he only had an 8th Grade education. Fuertes stepped in and asked the school to reconsider, and they did. Joe attended the Art Institute and met Mary, and thus began their adventure together.

Joe and Mary got engaged in 1931 and married in 1933. One trip out West to Glacier National Park with her father and her sister was all it took for Mary to understand the appeal of Wyoming, and Mary and Joe soon made plans to move to the Winds. They bought a 1929 grey Buick and moved in with her sister to save additional money. At the end of April, 1935, Mary and Joe left Chicago in the Buick, which was modified with cupboards under the dashboard, and seats that folded down to create a double bed. They camped in the Dubois area and looked for work in the Upper Winds and in the Teton area, with Joe securing a gig as a guide. After camping in Yellowstone and catching more cutthroat trout than they could eat, the couple went to Dubois to get settled in.

Their first year, the Backs tried to make their living off of their art, but the two soon realized they could not—at least not at that point. An old friend of Joe's named Elmer Davies agreed to be a partner in a dude ranch, and the Coopers bought Lava Creek Ranch, 22 miles west of Dubois, for $1,500. With Davies, they built three cabins and renamed it the Rocker Y Ranch. The going was rough. Mary and Joe lost their only child in childbirth, and Mary's recuperation was slow. The 1938 dude ranch season was a bust for them, and their focus turned to the

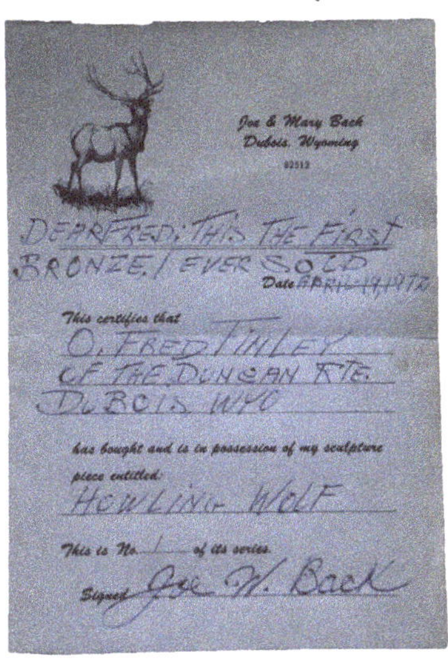

The receipt (top) and sculpture (bottom) that was the first bronze Joe Back sold, in the collection of John Finley.

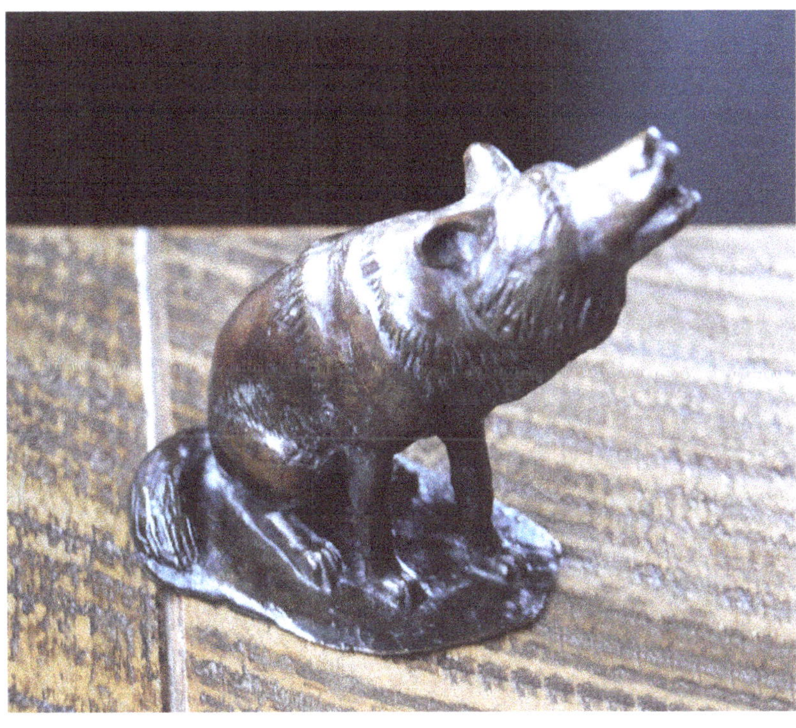

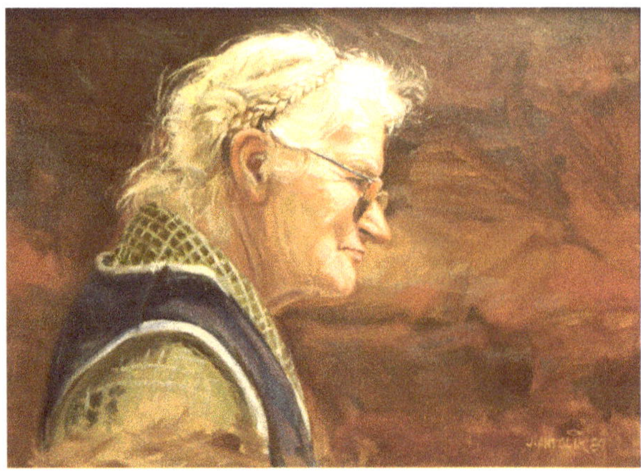

"Mary," by Jerry Antolik.

next summer's possibilities. Happily, 1939 brought more guests than they could house, with at least one person sleeping under the stars most weeks. But the partnership with Davies was not proving amicable. The Backs sold their half of the ranch to Davies, and bought Gordon Shippen's place, which was seven miles closer to Dubois, in the shadow of the Ramshorn Peak. A new era of dude ranching seemed to be opening up for the Backs, but ominous events in Europe—signs of war--spooked potential guests, and 1940 was a somewhat disappointing season.

The Backs increasingly looked outward, beyond their cozy cabin. Their baby's death was a terrible blow, but the Backs found comfort in community. In 1940 the first high school opened in Dubois, with 30 students, and the Backs hosted a post-Christmas party for the students. Mary became the Dubois town librarian, and she became a skilled carpenter. Joe earned money in a dozen different ways, from sawing timber to leading hunting parties. The dude season passed fruitfully in 1941, then on Dec. 7, war came to the Wind River Valley, and to the rest of the United States.

Not only were the Backs worried about their country, they were also nearly out of business. No

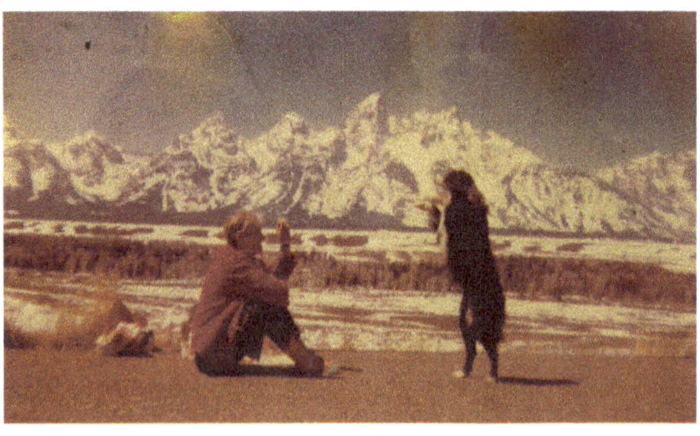

Mary training her dog Buttons with a view of the Tetons

one was taking dude ranch vacations during wartime. Joe took a job as a
welder building ships in Oakland, doing his part for the war effort (and
for the Backs' financial solvency), and Mary followed after him once she
found a caretaker for the Rocker Y. She secured work as a mechanic for
United Airlines, and the couple lived in San Francisco. Unfortunately,
their caretaker at the ranch quit and a replacement was not found, and the
Backs were forced to return to Wyoming. They still needed work, so they
ended up in Cheyenne, where United was looking for workers. Cheyenne
did not excite them, but the two had more time to make art there, and Joe
delved deeply into painting. In 1944, the Backs once again found that
their attention was needed on the ranch, and they returned home for good.
Joe's sculptures of animals were selling well, and the couple focused on
production of these small models. The war ended, promising a rebound of
the dude business. But chest pains precipitated a visit by Joe to the doctor in
Lander, and they received the news that he needed to slow down if he hoped
to live a long life. The couple decided to get out of the dude wrangling
business with all of its strenuous activity, and concentrate on art.

Joe and Mary Back—but especially Mary—were incalculably influential
in the art world of postwar Wyoming. They were not rich patrons, or
internationally known artists with big exhibitions in major cities. They
were on the ground, nurturing the inspiration and abilities of people like
them. The Backs were a living example of how the role of the Wind River
Mountains changed in Wyoming history, from an unforgiving, wild place

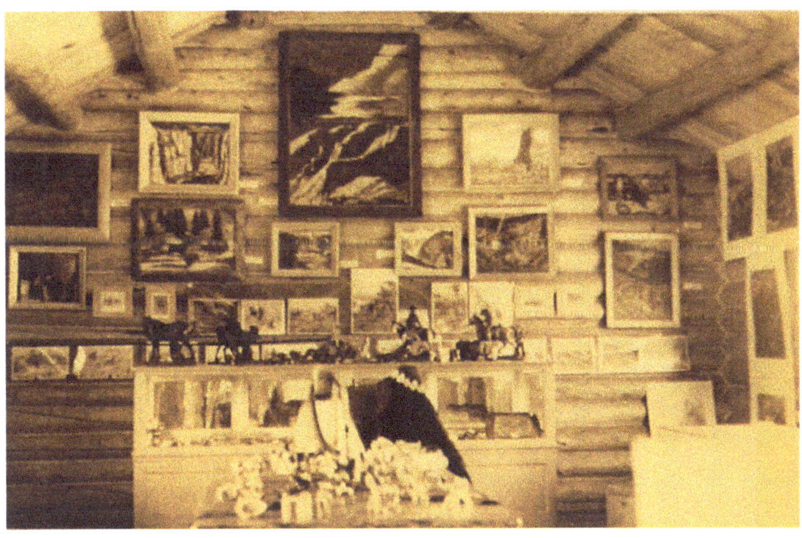

Inside the Back store on Highway 26.

to….well, an unforgiving, wild place that is appreciated precisely for its relatively untouched, fierce beauty. Although ranchers to this day still run cattle (and some sheep) in the Winds, the dude ranches—aided by the railroad—opened up Wyoming to Americans across the continent. The dude wranglers knew that the breathtaking landscapes were one of the biggest draws. Mary and Joe Back, as artists, hunters, and residents, appreciated and understood the beauty of the Winds and its wildlife better than most anyone. Their true love was art-making. The decision to stop hosting visitors at the Rocker Y was based partially on Joe's health, but it was enabled by the Backs' art.

As Lamb writes in *Mary's Way,* "…Mary's life got even busier as the painting classes continued to expand. Crowheart, on the Indian reservation brought together 13 folks for a Friday night gathering, to paint, exhibit, and talk painting. By 1954, more sites were added and Mary acknowledged, 'It looks like I'll be running around all winter.' She became a familiar sight on Wyoming roads, a miniature art wagon, with Mary at the wheel. While it was a chore for her to get to the several hundred students she had reached by then, it was no easier for some of the fledgling artists who rode horseback or drove Jeeps or station wagons for many miles to get to the

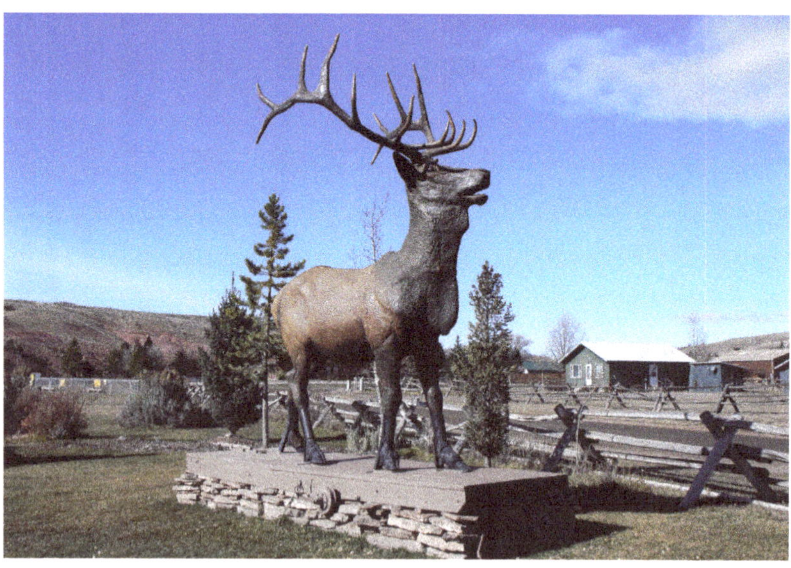

The giant elk sculpture Joe Back made to stop traffic in front of their gallery/store on Highway 26 just southeast of Dubois, Wyoming. It now sits at the front entrance of the KOA Campground.

classes. Art was definitely flourishing in the Wyoming back country, and Mary was right in the middle of it."

The Backs sold the Rocker Y Ranch and bought some land about 2 ½ miles east of Dubois, right along the Wind River. They set up their homestead to encourage traffic on the highway to stop by their home and studio to purchase art. Mary kept herself busy by teaching anyone and everyone. "Mary Back taught every little kid that was interested in art," John Finley recalls. "My dad took art lessons from Mary, and my oldest brother would stop in and visit Joe and help him do things around the studio. I remember her well. She could be tough, but everybody loved her."

Mary Back was a force to be reckoned with, and aside from nurturing the love of art-making in kids and adults within reach of her and her vehicle, she started the Wind River Valley Artists' Guild (WRVAG) in 1954 after successfully hosting a perennial summer exhibition of work. With her at the helm, the guild took off, and it remains vital today.

The exhibition was not initially centered in Dubois, however. "In the first years of the WRVAG until the late '80s the show went around the county, to Lander, Riverton, and Dubois," says Twila Blakeman, the mayor of Dubois and a close friend of the Backs. "Finally it settled up here, and she was such an influence. When Joe decided to stop outfitting and do his artwork, a lot of the natives questioned if he was going to make a living doing those little animals. They'd say, 'You can't, nobody would buy them.' He proved them wrong. And now, artists, including those who have moved here since then, are drawn to the beauty, yes—but also because Joe and Mary made it such a mecca for art."

In 1957, the WRVAG exhibition attracted 340 entries, and the association has received paintings from as far away as Afghanistan. Consider this: The show is based in a town that had 177 residents in 1930 and still may not have broken the 1,000-person barrier. The Backs are responsible for this, particularly Mary. "Yes, the arts are more active around here because the Backs founded the guild," says Tammy Lucas, the president of the WRVAG. "They donated a lot of their artwork, and when they passed away, they left all their money to the Wind River Valley Artists' Guild. And now we are in our 68th year. To this day, it's not a juried show. Anybody can enter, and that was the Back's idea. The guild's exhibition brings a lot of people to town. The people around here love coming to the art show; they're able to connect with the artists. It's very good for Dubois to have it here."

Lucas, who is married to artist Tom Lucas, is also manager of Headwaters Arts & Conference Center, a facility at the western end of Dubois. The concept of a building to house art exhibitions, lessons, and similar meetings came out of the need to house the WRVAG annual exhibition, and Back money helped get the idea going. The current facility (a drafty concrete building had previously served to house the WRVAG) opened in the winter of 1996. Joe Back died in 1986. Mary carried on, even as she described the loss of her husband as a sort of amputation, "cutting off half of me." She continued to teach and to hike the badlands, Absarokas, and her beloved Wind River Mountains.

In a letter dated October 4, 1988, Mary described a backcountry trip up to the Continental Divide in the upper Winds. She'd made this backpacking trip often, but now, in her 80s, she couldn't carry her pack. So she enlisted the use of a goat. "Mine was a big white tannenberg goat named Jupiter," Mary wrote. "He carried my whole load, and was a lovely companion. I didn't have to lead him. He and the others just walked along with us, quieter than dogs, but wearing those ironic goatly expressions that implied they were laughing at us all the way."

She received the Governor's Award for Service to the Arts, with the

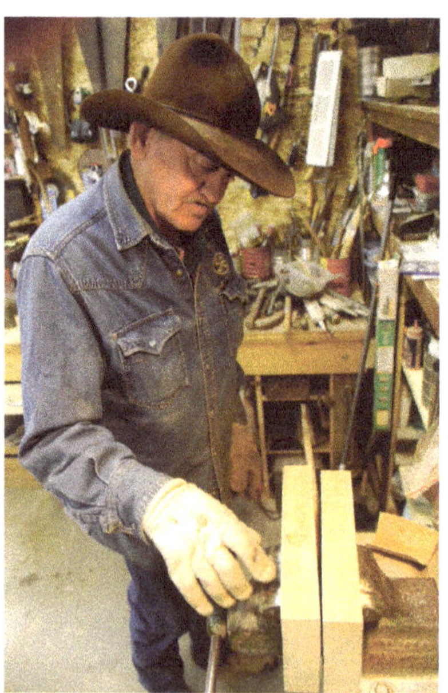

Tom Lucas

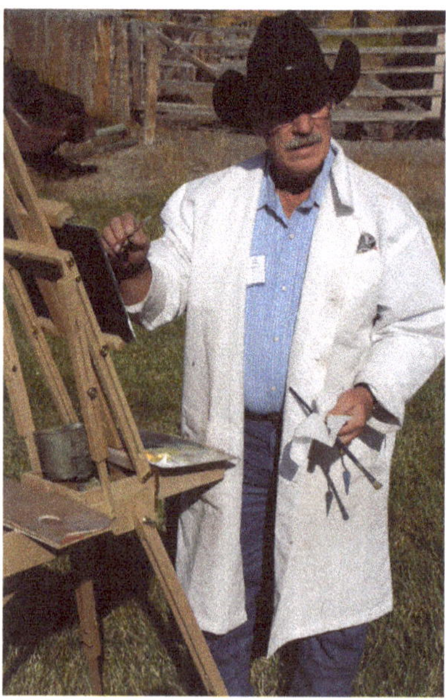

Lee Cable

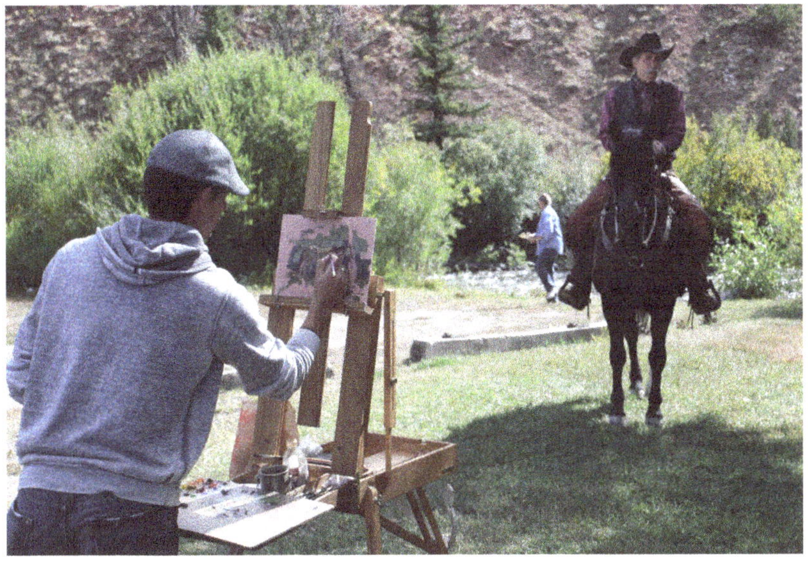

John Phelps posing for an SKB artist.

proclamation reading, in part, "Whereas, her interest, support and promotion
of the arts in Wyoming has continued through her numerous volunteer
activities including her work with the International Wind River Art Show,
which is the direct result of her years of teaching in Fremont County;
and whereas, when the Wind River Artists' Guild was formed, Mary was
president for the first three years, and she continues to work, paint, exhibit,
and help with the annual show held in Dubois in August; and whereas,
recognizing Mary's work over the years and her contributions toward
enhancing all forms of art and inspiring students to work in their own
particular styles, she, along with her husband, Joe, was awarded Central
Wyoming College's Medallion of Honor in 1982; now, therefore, I, Mike
Sullivan, Governor of the State of Wyoming, bestow the 1987 Governor's
Award for the Arts for Service to the Arts to Mary Back, recognizing her as
a leader within the arts field, locally and statewide, as well as recognizing
her ongoing, tireless efforts in promotion of the arts in Wyoming."

Mary passed away May 28, 1991, at the age of 86.

It's not hard to find people in the Winds who remember Mary, and think
of her and Joe with a wistful smile. It is difficult to express her impact on
the people she knew. Consider Lyndie Anne Duff, who arrived in Dubois a
little lost, and walked with Mary in the mornings, worked in the studio with
her, went to church with her--"a devoted disciple of Mary's way." She said,

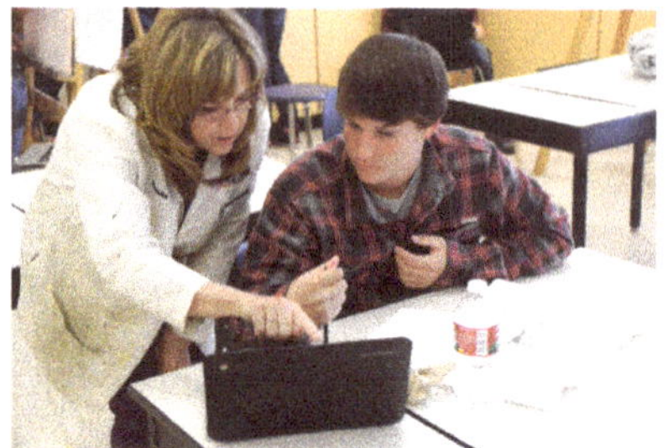

Wanda Mumm with student

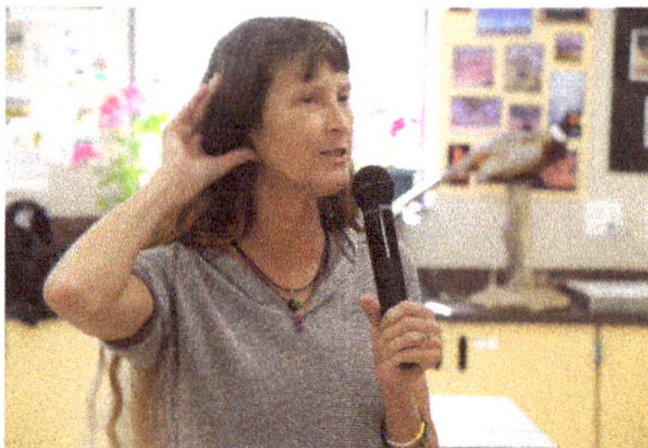

Danita Sayers

"Mary is like living bread—she is salty and deep like the sea. We speak of Mary in the present because Mary will always be with those who love her and, through her book, with others."

A scant six years separated the opening of Headwaters Arts & Conference Center and the arrival of another energetic force in the visual art world around the Wind River Mountains. In 2000, an artist named Susan Kathleen Black passed away after a long illness. Her husband, Jim Parkman, wanted to honor Black's memory in a way that kept her generous art-spirit alive. One of her friends, Pam Dean Cable, suggested to Parkman that he put his effort toward art education, because Black so thoroughly enjoyed and benefited from workshops and lessons in her growth from a flight attendant

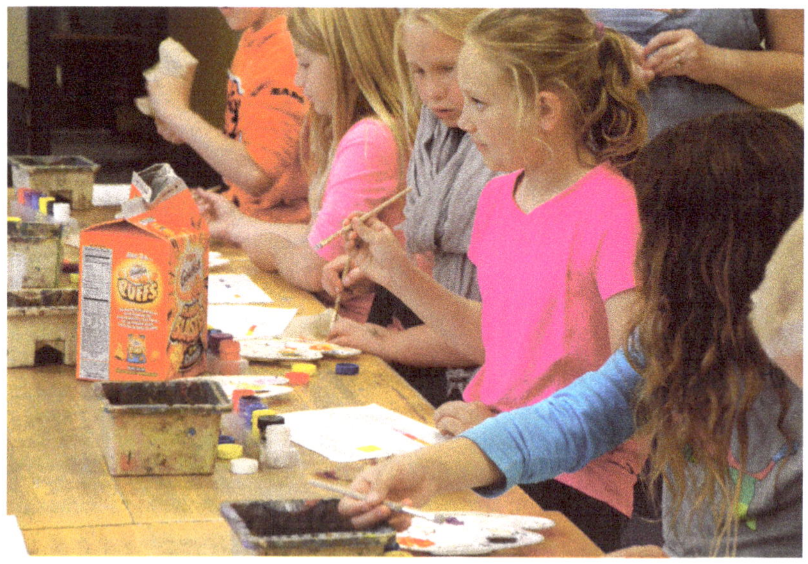

Dubois students working on color charts.

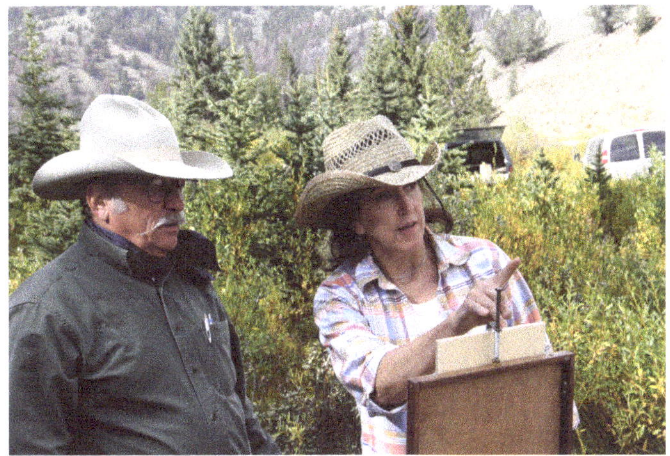

Jeannie Mackenzie helps an SKB participant

interested in art to a floral and wildlife artist with exhibitions across the country.

Parkman, a Houston businessman who understands how to get things done and how to delegate, immediately asked Cable to pursue her idea, and in 2001, an early version of the Susan Kathleen Black Foundation hosted a workshop for wildlife painters in Divide, Colorado. The event was a success, but Cable, along with her husband, the painter Lee Cable, and a close friend of Black's named Claudia Lampe, felt a better location could be found for the event.

Just earlier, Lee Cable met John Phelps, a Dubois hunting guide and artist, at a wildlife art show in Tulsa, and the two bonded over their mutual love of horses, painting, and campfire tales. Phelps invited Lee to visit Dubois and go on a pack trip up in the Winds, near Gannett Peak. The artists Greg Beecham, Gary Keimig, and Joe Arnold joined them, and Phelps organized the mule train and came up with a rough itinerary.

It was an eventful eight days featuring spooked horses, a farrier with a broken arm, paint boxes lost over cliffs, horses bleeding from bucking through a boulder field, and a nighttime bareback ride over a swollen Torrey Creek on a temperamental Appaloosa. Phelps recalls throwing a pack saddle into the fire in anger. Lee was overheard whispering to his horse at the end, "Sandy, if you just get into this trailer I will never bring you back to this godforsaken country again."

The ruggedness of the land may be tough on a horse, but it fascinates humans. Phelps and Lee simply chose to ride their horses in the Absarokas in future years, and Lee reported back to his wife that he might have found a home for the SKB workshop. The Headwaters facility was a good fit for SKB, and the annual event took off. But the Cables live in Colorado, Jim Parkman is in Houston, and other key figures in SKB live in far-flung places from Ohio to Montana to Maryland and down to Florida. Why does the event always return to the Winds?

"The Headwaters Center—right on the Wind River—is the perfect venue for the SKB event," says Pam Cable, SKB's executive director. "The area is a nature artist's dreamscape! We couldn't believe our collective good fortune when we discovered it. There were the obvious grand landscapes, of course, but also limitless small hidden treasures to be discovered among the flora and fauna waiting for an artist to interpret with paint and brush. To say that Dubois, Headwaters, and the Wind River Valley are a home away from home cannot be overstated. Nearly 2,000 SKB artists have gathered here over the years to thank Nature for her gifts by interpreting the essence of those gifts each in their own unique ways. Be it an awe-inspiring landscape, indigenous creatures big or small, a cluster of stones, a flower, bird, or bug—all deserve and get the attention of an artist."

SKB certainly seems to be of the same spirit as the Backs. Although the SKB workshop (now called a Rendezvous) is in the Winds for just one week a year, its impact is wider. The participants paint the scenery of the area and thus continue to spread appreciation for the Wind River mountains and valley and their beauty. But it goes further--before the Rendezvous, several SKB instructors arrive in Dubois early to spend three days working with the students at the Dubois public school, which teaches kids K-12. SKB sponsors or runs art education projects all over the United States, but it is likely that the organization's work in Dubois is the closest in spirit to what Mary Back did and cared about—and not just because it's happening in Dubois. Teaching kids about art opens their eyes to see the world more fully, creates future art collectors, and gives the children another way to express themselves. The SKB instructors work on fundamentals during that pre-workshop blitz at the Dubois school, and then, during the workshop, one morning is set aside so all the participants in the Rendezvous can help inspire the local kids. It's called Mentor Day, and it is usually held on EA Ranch.

Participants in Susan K. Black's Dubois workshops go out of their way to state that Mentor Day is a big deal for them—both students and mentors.

The results often indicate significant artistic development on the part of the kids—or at least significantly boosted enthusiasm about painting. SKB has been mentoring Dubois students for more than nine years now, and word has gotten around. It helps that art students from Dubois have won more than half of the blue ribbons in the statewide competition for the last few years. The young Dubois artists have always been interested in seeing that the professional painters and sculptors at SKB make a life of making art. They receive the knowledge that the creation of art is a viable lifestyle. They are taken seriously by people who make art for a living.

"What Danita [Sayers, the art teacher at the Dubois public school] does with the students is just amazing," says SKB instructor Wanda Mumm. "She knows how to handle them and how to give them what they need. But sometimes kids need to hear the same thing from another person. The SKB Mentor Program also allows the kids to zero in on what they need help on. The students aren't just interested in an experience with SKB artists anymore. Now they have a specific goal. It may be to learn more about painting nocturnes or clouds. This is a shift. They realize that this is an opportunity to get help outside the classroom."

The SKB instructors get reports that the Mentor Program has acted as a catalyst to get some of the students going on a yearlong project or goal. "What happens on one Mentor Day can be a big influence," Mumm says.

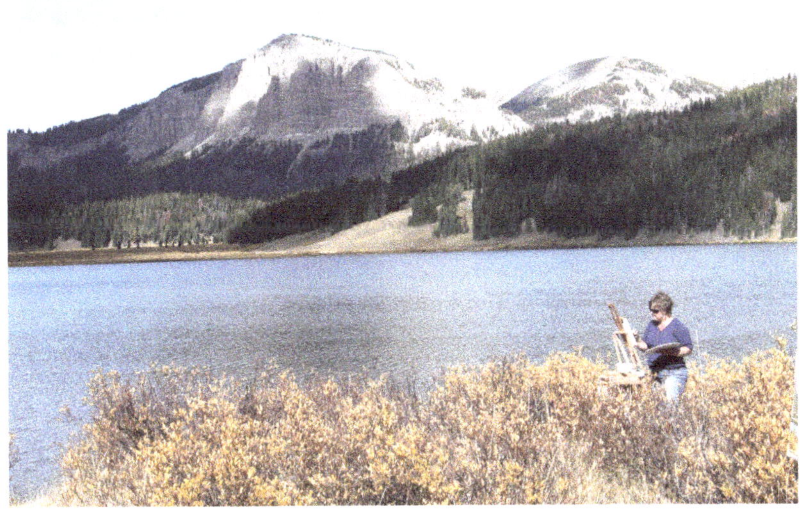

SKB artist painting at Brooks Lake.

"They get advice, information, and inspiration that can carry through the whole year."

Alfred Jacob Miller, from Philadelphia. Albert Bierstadt and Carl Rungius, from Germany. Mary Back from Vermont and Joe Back from Ohio. SKB instructors from Louisiana, Michigan, California, England, Colorado, and Canada. Artists from all over, cross-pollinating ideas with indigenous people, Wyoming artists, and residents of the Wind River mountains and valleys…it's still going on, thousands of years after the first petroglyphs were pecked. From simple stone tools of prehistory to today's laptops in a Dubois classroom, visual art has wonderfully conveyed, portrayed, or been influenced by the crags and pines, the bears and elk, the people and places of the Winds.

"Everybody likes it there," Phelps simply states. "They are used to it—they know the places to go to paint. From Brooks Lake to Torrey Canyon, it's home." Ω

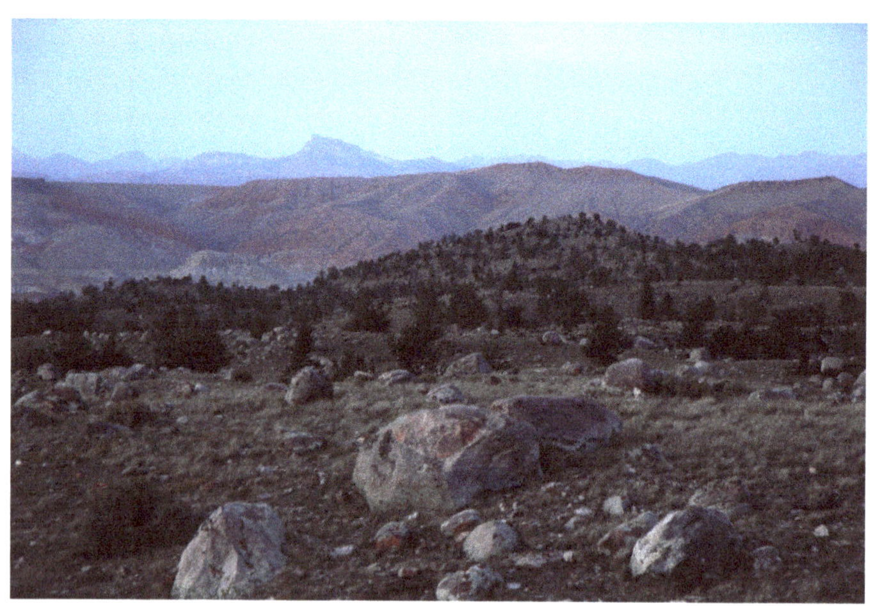

Bibliography

Personal interview with Stephen V. Banks, Dubois historian and expert on Rocky Mountain trappers, July 2017.

Personal interview with Joe Brandl, outdoorsman and local historian in Dubois, Wyoming, May 2018.

Personal interview with Monie and John Finley, Dubois ranchers and artists, December 2017.

Personal interview with Clint Gilchrist, director of the Museum of the Mountain Man, July 2017.

Personal interview with Peter Hassrick, director emeritus of the Buffalo Bill Center of the West, July 2017.

Personal interview with Tom Lucas, artist and Dubois historian, July 2017.

Personal interview with Sig Schulz, Dubois resident and tie hack historian, December 2017.

Personal interview with Bonnie Lawrence-Smith, archaeologist and staff member at Draper Museum, at the Buffalo Bill Center of the West, in Cody, Wyoming, May 2018.

Personal interview with Willie St. Clair, Shoshone elder, May 2018.

Personal interview with Tory Taylor, guide and Dubois historian, July 2017.

Personal interview with Johanna Thompson, geologist, July 2017.

Allison, Mary. *Dubois Wyoming Area History,* Curtis Media Corporation, 1991.

Biddle, Nicholas. *The Journals of Lewis & Clark.* Heritage Press, 1962.

Burt, Matthew Struthers. *The Diary of a Dude Wrangler.* Charles Scribners Sons, 1938.

Cable, Pam Dean. *Susan K. Black: An Artistic Heart.* James E. Parkman, 2003.

Carhart, Arthur. *Hi, Stranger! The Complete Guide to Dude Ranches.* Ziff-Davis Publishing Co., 1949.

Cartwright, David W. *Natural History of Western Wild Animals and Guide for Hunters, Trappers, and Sportsmen.* Blade Printing & Paper Co., 1875.

Coyner, David H. *The Lost Trappers: A Collection of Interesting Scenes and Events in the Rocky Mountains.* E. D. Truman, 1850.

Ewers, John C. *Artists of the Old West.* Chanticleer Press/Doubleday & Co., 1965.

Francis, Julie E. and Loendorf, Lawrence L. *Ancient Visions: Petroglyphs and Pictographs of the Wind River and Bighorn Country, Wyoming and Montana.* University of Utah Press, 2002.

Frison, George C., Andrews, R. L., Adovasio, J. M., Carlisle, R. C. and Edgar, Robert. "A Late Paleoindian Animal Trapping Net from Northern Wyoming," in *American Antiquity* Vol. 51, No. 2 (Apr., 1986), pp. 352-361. Cambridge University Press.

Goodman, Mark. *From the Broadax to the Railroad Tracks.* Wind River Historical Center.

Harris, Burton. *John Colter: His Years in the Rockies.* University of Nebraska Press, 1993.

Hassrick, Peter H. *Albert Bierstadt: Witness to a Changing West.* University of Oklahoma Press, 2018.

Hassrick, Peter H. *Drawn to Yellowstone: Artists in America's First National Park,* University of Washington Press, 2002.

Hendricks, Gordon. "The First Three Western Journeys of Albert Bierstadt."

The Art Bulletin, vol. 46, no. 3, 1964, pp. 333–365. *JSTOR,* www.jstor.org/stable/3048185.

Irving, Washington. *The Adventures of Captain Bonneville.* University of Oklahoma Press, 1961.

Johnson, Thomas Hoevet. "The Enos Family and Wind River Shoshone Society: A Historical Analysis." Ph.D. diss., University of Illinois at Urbana-Champaign, 1975.

Just, Emma. Personal letter from May 15, 1872.

Kroeber, A. L. "Decorative Symbolim of the Arapaho," in *American Anthropologist,* New Series, Vol. 3, No. 2, April-June 1901. Pp. 308-336.

Lamb, Ruth Mary. *Mary's Way: A Memoir of the Life of Mary Cooper Black,* FuturePrep, 1999.

"Vision Quest Structures," by Lawrence Loendorf. http://www.pryormountains.org/cultural-history/archaeology/vision-quest-structures/

McPhee, John. *Annals of the Former World.* Farrar, Strauss & Giroux, 1981.

Mercer, A. S. *The Banditti of the Plains.* Self-published, 1894.

Mumey, Nolie. *The Teton Mountains: Their History and Tradition.* The Artcraft Press, 1947.

Pinkerton, Joan Trego. *Knights of the Broadax: The Story of the Wyoming Tie Hack.* Prong Horn Press, 2016.

Raynolds, W. F. "Exploration of the Yellowstone River." Surveying report published by the Government Printing Office, 1868.

Rosenberg, Robert and Elizabeth. "The Warm Spring Canyon Tie Flume," on www.WyomingHistory.org.

Ross, Marvin C. *The West of Alfred Jacob Miller.* University of Oklahoma Press, 1951.

Russell, Carl P. *Firearms, Traps & Tools of the Mountain Men.* Alfred A. Knopf, 1967.

Schaldach, William J. *Carl Rungius, Big Game Painter: Fifty Years With Brush and Rifle.* The Countryman Press, 1945.

Shimkin, D. B. "Dynamics of Recent Wind River Shoshone History, *American Anthropologist,* Vol. 44, Issue 3, July-September 1942. Pp. 451-462.

Shimkin, D. B. *Wind River Shoshone Ethnogeography.* University of California Press, Berkeley and Los Angeles, 1947.

Strong, Lisa Maria. *Images of Indian-White Contact in the Watercolors of Alfred Jacob Miller, 1837-60.* Columbia University, 1998.

Taylor, Tory. *On the Trail of the Mountain Shoshone Sheep Eaters: A High Latitude Archaeological Odyssey.* Wind River Publishing, 2017.

Topping, Eugene Sayre. *The Chronicles of the Yellowstone.* Pioneer Press Co., 1888.

Trenton, Patricia and Hassrick, Peter H. *The Rocky Mountains: A Vision for Artists in the 19th Century,* University of Oklahoma Press, 1983.

Tyler, Ross. Essay in *Alfred Jacob Miller: Artist as Explorer,* Gerald Peters Gallery, Santa Fe, 1999.

Vinton, Stallo. *John Colter: Discoverer of Yellowstone Park.* Edward Eberstadt, 1926.

Weeks, Rupert. *Pachee Goyo: History and Legends From the Shoshone.* Jelm Mountain Press, 1961.

100 Years of Artist Activity in Wyoming. University of Wyoming Art Museum.

"Dude Ranches Out West," guidebook published in 1931 by the Union Pacific Rail Road Co.

"The Dude Rancher," the newsletter of the Dude Rancher's Association, multiple issues, 1929-1947.

"The Wind River Reservation Yesterday and Today: The Legends—The

Land—The People," pamphlet, Curriculum Development Workshop, Wind River Reservation

www nativePartnership.org (aka American Indian Relief Council)

INDEX

Back, Mary and Joe 39-40, 107-8, 115-25, 128, 130
Banks, Stephen V. 26, 28-32, 52, 60, 71, 73
Bell, Cleve 65-6
Bierstadt, Albert 18, 23, 33-5, 87, 89-95, 130
Black, Susan Kathleen 41-2, 126-7
Bonneville, Benjamin Louis Eulalie de 21, 70, 78
Bridger, Jim 83-4, 96
Burt, Maxwell Struthers 6, 17, 60, 103, 106

Cable, Pam 42, 126-128
Catlin, George 18-9, 85
Champlain, Samuel 31
Colter, John 72-77

Finley, John 9-11, 16, 20, 101, 115, 123
Finley, Monie 10-11
Frost, Francis Seth 33

Hassrick, Peter H. 19, 33-4, 90-3

Lewis & Clark 71-5
Loendorf, Lawrence 26, 48-9, 51
Love, David 11
Lucas, Tammy 123-4
Lucas, Tom 27-8, 43, 124

McPhee, John 11, 13-6
Miller, Alfred Jacob 32-4, 68, 79-86, 91, 130
Moran, Thomas 35-6, 94, 95-6
Moore, Charlie 100-1

Olson, Martin 108, 110-11, 114-5

Parkman, Jim 41-2, 126-8
Parrish, Maxfield 17
Phelps, John 42, 68-70, 125, 127-8, 130

Pleissner, Ogden 37-9, 101-3, 109

Raynolds, William F.
Rocky Mountain Rendezvous 30, 32, 80-1, 83-4, 86, 92, 128
Roosevelt, Theodore 38, 99
Ross, Marvin C. 32, 86
Rungius, Carl 36, 38-9, 100-2, 109, 130

Smith, Bonnie 53, 55-6
Stewart, Sir William Drummond 32, 79-81, 87, 89

Taylor, Tory 25-6, 48, 51, 56, 108
tie hacks 35, 37, 107, 108-16

Vérendrye, François and Louis-Joseph de la 31, 68-9

Washakie 50, 57, 61-3, 100
Water Ghost Woman 26, 45-6
Wind River Valley Artists Guild 21, 40, 123

Layout by Peggy Kinstler
Cover design by Sean Berthelot
Photos by Bob Bahr
Much thanks to the Susan Kathleen Black Foundation for
crucial funding for this book.